Adams Chemist
150 Crookes,
Sheffield
S10 1UH

HORSE RIDER'S YEARBOOK

David & Charles

A DAVID & CHARLES BOOK

First published in the UK in 2004

Copyright © David & Charles 2004

Distributed in North America
by F&W Publications, Inc.
4700 East Galbraith Road
Cincinnati, OH 45236
1-800-289-0963

David & Charles has asserted the right to be identified as author of this work
in accordance with the Copyright, Designs and Patents Act, 1988.

All rights reserved. No part of this publication may be reproduced,
stored in a retrieval system, or transmitted, in any form or by any means, electronic
or mechanical, by photocopying, recording or otherwise, without prior permission in
writing from the publisher.

Every effort has been made to trace the copyright owners of all extracts.
Any ommissions wil be corrected in a subsequent printing if the publishers
are informed.

Extract from *Venus Observed* by Christopher Fry reproduced by kind permission
of Oxford University Press.
Extract from *Four-Year-Old* by Edric Roberts reproduced by kind permission of
The Field magazine.

All photographs by HORSEPIX, except main image front cover by Kit Houghton.

A catalogue record for this book is available from the British Library.

ISBN 0 7153 1807 1

Printed in Singapore by KHL Printing Co Pte Ltd
for David & Charles
Brunel House Newton Abbot Devon

Commissioning Editor: Jane Trollope
Designer: Lisa Forrester
Desk Editor: Shona Wallis
Text supplied and edited by Jo Weeks
Production Controller: Ros Napper

Visit our website at www.davidandcharles.co.uk

David & Charles books are available from all good bookshops; alternatively you can
contact our Orderline on (0)1626 334555 or write to us at FREEPOST EX2110,
David & Charles Direct, Newton Abbot, TQ12 4ZZ (no stamp required UK mainland).

Whilst utmost care has been taken in compiling the facts/information in this diary,
the Publishers cannot accept responsibility for any errors.

CONTENTS

Personal details

About me	4–5

My details, my vet and equine dentist, electrical safety

About my horses	6–11

Body protectors, riding hats, rugs, microchipping, clothes sizes, conversion charts

Getting organized	12–15

Year planner and worming calendar

A record of my costs	16–17

Essential information

Points of the horse	18–19

Basic anatomy and skeleton

Teeth	20–21

When to call the dentist, ageing your horse

First aid for horses	22–25

Vital signs, initial care, bandaging and poulticing

First aid for people	26–27

What to do in an emergency

Horse health	28–31

A guide to horse ailments

Road safety	32–33

Riding on the road, transporting your horse

Feeding your horse	34–37

Nutrition, concentrates, forage

Perfect pastures	38–41

Paddock care, poisonous plants, grasses

Ideal stable	42

Yard and stable design

Perfect manège	43

The site, some schooling figures

Feet and shoeing	44–45

Foot care and problems, a well-shod horse

Saddles	46–47

Measuring your horse and fitting a saddle

Bridles	48–49

Fitting bridles, martingales and bits

A guide to riding terms	50–51

Some definitions, a guide to terms

Diary	54–117
My notes	118–119
Useful addresses	120–121

4 USEFUL INFORMATION

About me

Name

Address

Phone home/work

Mobile

Email

Driving licence number/car registration

Trailer/lorry serial numbers

Passport number/renewal date

National insurance number

Blood group

Breakdown assistance membership

Hat size

Glove size

Shoe size/calf height and width

Jacket size

Jodphur size/leg length

Body protector size

Useful phone numbers

Livery yard

Vet

Farrier

Equine dentist

Doctor

Dentist

Complementary therapist

Equine insurer

Local police station

Feed merchant

Forage merchant

Bedding merchant

Riding school/instructor

Rug cleaner/repairer

ABOUT ME 5

Saddler/tack shop
Tack repairer
Builder/carpenter
Bridleways officer/park ranger(s)
Equine charity(ies)
Car insurer (and policy number)
Property insurer (and policy number)
Others

Your vet
- Get to know your vet before you need him or her in an emergency. Even with a very healthy horse, your vet will need to visit once a year to give vaccinations. You should get on well and be able to discuss any concerns about your horse's health. If you feel you aren't on the same wavelength, consider changing vets – sooner rather than later.
- If you keep your horse at a livery yard, make sure the owner has your vet's name and contact number and is aware of any important information about your horse's health.

Your equine dentist
- Your vet may be able to look after your horse's teeth, otherwise ask him or her to recommend a good dentist.
- See p.20 for information about dental treatment.

Electrical safety
When using electrical equipment, such as clippers, near horses always practise extreme care:

✔ Check the equipment, particularly the flex, and use a circuit breaker plug – every single time you use it.

✔ Ensure the flex is well out of the way of the horse's hooves and teeth.

✔ Ensure you, your hands, the horse and the area you are in are all dry.

✔ If you suspect electrocution, switch off the electric supply or use dry wood, such as a broom handle, to remove the electric equipment from the person (see also 'First aid for people', p.26).

What is microchipping?
Microchipping involves inserting a small microchip under the skin of your horse's neck. It causes no discomfort to him and means he is easily reunited with you should he go missing or be stolen.

6 USEFUL INFORMATION

About

Age

Height

Sex

Breed

Colour

Face markings

Leg and feet markings

Other distinctive marks

Saddle size and length, make, serial number

Bridle size

Rug size

Passport life number

Heart rate

Temperature

Respiration rate

Weight

Freeze mark

Microchip

Insurance policy number

Date of purchase

History

Previous owner and how long they owned him/her

Sire/dam

Breed registration certificate number

ABOUT MY HORSES

Body protectors

Buying a body protector
- Measurements you will need: waist, chest, waist-to-waist – from waist at the back, over your shoulder to waist at the front.
- Choose the correct size using the charts supplied with all BETA (British Equine Trade Association) standard protectors.
- Try on the protector over light clothing – heavier clothing is best over the top.
- Adjust to fit closely, using the straps and fastenings.
- Wear it for about 5 minutes in the shop to ensure it is still comfortable when it has moulded to your body shape.

Does it fit?
✔ It reaches your breastbone at the front and the base of your neck at the back.
✔ It fits around your body.
✔ It finishes just below your ribs (2.5cm/1in) at the front.
✔ It covers your collar bones.
✔ It wouldn't push up at the back (too long) when you sit in the saddle.
✔ It is comfortable in all riding positions – try these out as far as possible in the shop before you buy.

BETA 2000 Standard in brief

Level 1 (black label)
Low level of protection for licensed jockeys only.

Level 2 (brown label)
For use in low-risk situations only. NOT for jumping, riding on roads, riding young horses, riding excitable horses. NOT for inexperienced riders.

Level 3 (purple label)
Appropriate for normal horse riding and competitions.

Riding hats

To find your size measure the circumference of your head, just above your ears, preferably using a tape marked with centimetres. Choose hats that meet at least one of the following safety standards – BSEN1384 (British Standards Institute) or PAS015 or ASTM F1163/SEI (American Society for Testing and Materials/Safety Equipment Institute). New hats have an easy-to-understand star rating to ensure you pick the most suitable for you.

Size guide

Head size (cm)	Riding hat	Jockey skull
51	6¼	00
52	6⅜	00½
53	6½	0
54	6⅝	0½
55	6¾	1
56	6⅞	1½
57	7	2
58	7⅛	2½
59	7¼	3
60	7¼	3½
61	7½	4
62	7⅝	4½
63	7¾	5

What size rug or blanket?

Get a tape measure and place one end in the middle of your horse's chest. Get someone to take the other end around his side, holding it at the same level, to the middle of his back legs, below the top of the tail. Rug sizes are in increments of 3 inches – for example 51in, 54in, 57in. If your horse falls between increments, a rug that is slightly too large is usually better than one that is slightly too small. Some rugs are fuller than others, or more adjustable. Look carefully before you buy as few places will exchange rugs.

USEFUL INFORMATION

About

Age

Height

Sex

Breed

Colour

Face markings

Leg and feet markings

Other distinctive marks

Saddle size and length, make, serial number

Bridle size

Rug size

Passport life number

Heart rate

Temperature

Respiration rate

Weight

Freeze mark

Microchip

Insurance policy number

Date of purchase

History

Previous owner and how long they owned him/her

Sire/dam

Breed registration certificate number

Shoe sizes

Children

UK	6	7	8	9	9½	10	11	12	12½	13	1	2	2½	3
Continental	23	24	25	26	27	28	29	30	31	32	33	34	35	36

Adult

UK	4	5	6	6½	7	8	9	9½	10	11	12
Continental	37	38	39	40	41	42	43	44	45	46	47

Clothes sizes

Men

UK	36	38	40	42	44	46
US	36	38	40	42	44	46
Continental	46	48	50	52	54	56

Women

UK	10	12	14	16	18	20
US	8	10	12	14	16	18
Continental	38	40	42	44	46	48

Children (these sizes are very approximate)

US	3	4	6	8	10
Height (cm)	100	110	120	130	155
Age	3–4	4–5	6–8	8–10	10–12

Linear conversions

To convert

inches to centimetres multiply by 2.54cm

centimetres to inches multiply by 0.3937

feet to metres multiply by 0.3048

metres to feet multiply by 3.2808

In these quick-reference conversions the figures have been rounded up or down.

ft/in	m/cm	cm	in	m	ft	hh	cm
1in	2.5cm	1cm	½in	1m	3¼ft	10	102
2in	5cm	2cm	¾in	2m	6½ft	10.2	107
3in	7.5cm	3cm	1¼in	3m	10ft	11	112
4in	10cm	4cm	1½in	4m	13ft	11.2	117
5in	12.5cm	5cm	2in	5m	16½ft	12	122
6in	15cm	6cm	2½in	6m	19½ft	12.2	127
1ft	30cm	7cm	2¾in	7m	23ft	13	132
1ft 6in	45cm	8cm	3in	8m	26¼ft	13.2	137
2ft	60cm	9cm	3½in	9m	29½ft	14	142
2ft 6in	75cm	10cm	4in	10m	33ft	14.2	148
3ft	90cm	11cm	4¼in	11m	36ft	15	153
3ft 6in	1.06m	12cm	4¾in	12m	39½ft	15.2	158
4ft	1.20m	13cm	5in	13m	42½ft	16	163
4ft 6in	1.40m	14cm	5½in	14m	46ft		
5ft	1.50m	15cm	6in	15m	49¼ft		
5ft 6in	1.65m	20cm	8in	20m	65½ft		
6ft	1.80m						

10 USEFUL INFORMATION

About

Age

Height

Sex

Breed

Colour

Face markings

Leg and feet markings

Other distinctive marks

Saddle size and length, make, serial number

Bridle size

Rug size

Passport life number

Heart rate

Temperature

Respiration rate

Weight

Freeze mark

Microchip

Insurance policy number

Date of purchase

History

Previous owner and how long they owned him/her

Sire/dam

Breed registration certificate number

ABOUT MY HORSES

Weight conversions

To convert

ounces to grams	multiply by 28.3494
grams to ounces	multiply by 0.0353
pounds to kilograms	multiply by 0.4536
kilograms to pounds	multiply by 2.2046

In these quick-reference conversions the figures have been rounded up or down.

ounces	grams
1oz	28g
2oz	56g
3oz	85g
4oz	113g
5oz	142g

grams	ounces
15g	½oz
20g	¾oz
30g	1oz
35g	1¼oz
40g	1½oz
45g	1½oz
50g	1¾oz

pounds	kilograms
1lb	0.45kg
2lb	0.90kg
3lb	1.4kg
4lb	1.8kg
5lb	2.25kg

kilograms	pounds
1kg	2lb4oz
2kg	4lb7oz
3kg	6lb10oz
4kg	8lb13oz
5kg	11lb

Liquid conversions

To convert

fluid ounces to millilitres	multiply by 28.4
millilitres to fluid ounces	multiply by 0.3519
pints to litres	multiply by 0.5682
litres to pints	multiply by 1.7598

In these quick-reference conversions the figures have been rounded up or down.

fluid ounces	litres
2fl/oz	57ml
4fl/oz	114ml
6fl/oz	170ml
8fl/oz	227ml
10fl/oz	280ml
20fl/oz	560ml

millilitres	fluid ounces
10ml	3½fl/oz
20ml	7fl/oz
30ml	10½fl/oz
40ml	14fl/oz
50ml	17½fl/oz

pints	litres
1pt	0.5l
2pt	1l
3pt	1.5l
4pt	2.25l
5pt	3l
10pt	5.5l

litres	pints
1l	2pt
2l	3½pt
3l	5pt
4l	7pt
5l	8¾pt

GETTING ORGANIZED

January
1S
2S
3M
4T
5W
6T
7F
8S
9S
10M
11T
12W
13T
14F
15S
16S
17M
18T
19W
20T
21F
22S
23S
24M
25T
26W
27T
28F
29S
30S
31M

February
1T
2W HAY x 15
3T
4F
5S WORMED
6S
7M
8T
9W
10T
11F
12S
13S
14M
15T
16W FARRIER
17T
18F
19S
20S
21M
22T
23W
24T
25F
26S
27S
28M

March
1T
2W
3T
4F
5S
6S
7M
8T
9W
10T
11F
12S
13S
14M
15T
16W
17T
18F
19S
20S
21M
22T
23W
24T
25F
26S
27S
28M
29T
30W
31T

Getting organized

Don't forget to include:

Shoeing – every 4–6 weeks, possibly more often in summer

Vet's visits for routine vaccinations – once a year for equine flu and tetanus

Dentist's visit – every 6 months

Saddler's visit – every 6 months/annually

Worming – at least 5 times a year (see 'A worming calendar', opposite)

Horse shows – fitness schedules and a preparation countdown

Your holiday – remember to organize someone to care for your horse well in advance

GETTING ORGANIZED

For 2006 - when swopping to summer grazing start from shed end and graze up the field!!

April
1F
2S
3S
4M
5T
6W
7T
8F
9S
10S
11M
12T
13W
14T
15F
16S
17S
18M
19T
20W
21T
22F
23S
24S
25M
26T
27W
28T
29F
30S

May
1S
2M
3T
4W
5T
6F
7S
8S
9M
10T
11W
12T
13F
14S
15S
16M
17T
18W
19T
20F
21S
22S
23M
24T
25W
26T
27F
28S
29S
30M
31T

June
1W
2T
3F
4S
5S
6M
7T
8W
9T
10F
11S
12S
13M
14T
15W
16T
17F
18S
19S
20M
21T
22W
23T
24F
25S
26S
27M
28T
29W
30T

A worming calendar

When?	What for?	What with?
Sep–Oct	tapeworm	pyrantel or praziquantel (eg Strongid-P, Equimax)
Nov–Dec	encysted small redworm, large redworm (larvae and adults), seat worm	fenbendazole (eg Panacur Equine Guard)
Nov–Dec, after frosts	bots	ivermectin (eg Eqvalan)
Feb	as Dec for vulnerable horses (*)	fenbendazole (eg Panacur Equine Guard)
Mar to Sep, every 4–13 weeks (**)	routine, grazing-season worming (***)	

(*)Youngsters or those on heavily grazed pasture. (**)Administer every 4–13 weeks, depending on wormer used. (***)Make a note of the wormer you use this year and change to another one for the grazing season next year. Rotate annually, not at each dose, so for example, in year 1 use ivermectin, year 2 fenbendazole, year 3 praziquantel with ivermectin, year 4 pyrantel, year 5 moxidectin.

GETTING ORGANIZED

July
1F
2S
3S
4M
5T
6W
7T
8F
9S
10S
11M
12T
13W
14T
15F
16S
17S
18M
19T
20W
21T
22F
23S
24S
25M
26T
27W
28T
29F
30S
31S

August
1M
2T
3W
4T
5F
6S
7S
8M
9T
10W
11T
12F
13S
14S
15M
16T
17W
18T
19F
20S
21S
22M
23T
24W
25T
26F
27S
28S
29M
30T
31W

September
1T
2F
3S
4S
5M
6T
7W
8T
9F
10S
11S
12M
13T
14W
15T
16F
17S
18S
19M
20T
21W
22T
23F
24S
25S
26M
27T
28W
29T
30F

Worming record
Record the date and brand/type you use.

1..
2..
3..
4..
5..
6..
7..
8..

About wormers

✔ Good hygiene, particularly removing manure from paddocks, is crucial to worm control (see p.38).

✔ Before worming, weigh your horse (p.34) to ensure you give the correct dose.

✔ Consider getting an annual worm count done on a manure sample to check your worming regime is working.

GETTING ORGANIZED

October
1S
2S
3M
4T
5W
6T
7F
8S
9S
10M
11T
12W
13T
14F
15S
16S
17M
18T
19W
20T
21F
22S
23S
24M
25T
26W
27T
28F
29S
30S
31M

November
1T
2W
3T
4F
5S
6S
7M
8T
9W
10T
11F
12S
13S
14M
15T
16W
17T
18F
19S
20S
21M
22T
23W
24T
25F
26S
27S
28M
29T
30W

December
1T
2F
3S
4S
5M
6T
7W
8T
9F
10S
11S
12M
13T
14W
15T
16F
17S
18S
19M
20T
21W
22T
23F
24S
25S
26M
27T
28W
29T
30F
31S

Below are the main drugs used in wormers; read the label to find out what your wormer contains

- Fenbendazol (Benzimidazole Group) kills large and small redworm, and the 5-day treatment will kill encysted small redworm. Doesn't kill tapeworm or bots, not hugely effective against lungworm. Lasts for 6 weeks.

- Praziquantel (Macrocyclic Lactone Group) kills tapeworm and all other worms when combined with ivermectin, as in the wormer Equimax, which lasts 8–10 weeks.

- Ivermectin (Macrocyclic Lactone Group) kills all worms except tapeworm. Lasts for 8 weeks.

- Moxidectin (Macrocyclic Lactone Group) kills all worms except tapeworm. May kill some encysted small redworm. Lasts for 13 weeks.

- Pyrantel (Pyrimidine Group) kills tapeworm when double dosed. Doesn't kill bots, lungworm, encysted small redworm. Lasts for 6 weeks.

A record of my costs

Keeping a record of all your costs and how they arose will enable you to improve your budgeting skills for next year as well as build up a history of your horse for future reference. It might also show you where you could cut down or improve efficiency.

	Date	Details	Cost
Feed/forage			
		total	
Bedding			
		total	
Livery			
		total	
Dentist			
		total	

	Date	Details	Cost
Vet			
		total	

	Date	Details	Cost
Farrier			
		total	

	Date	Details	Cost
Other specialists			
		total	

Other expenditure	Include here all other items: insurance, riding lessons, wormers, rugs, saddle and rug repairs, new grooming kit, riding clothes, horsey treats, riding club and magazine subscriptions, entry and transport to competitions, clipping fees.		
		total	
	grand total		

Points of the horse

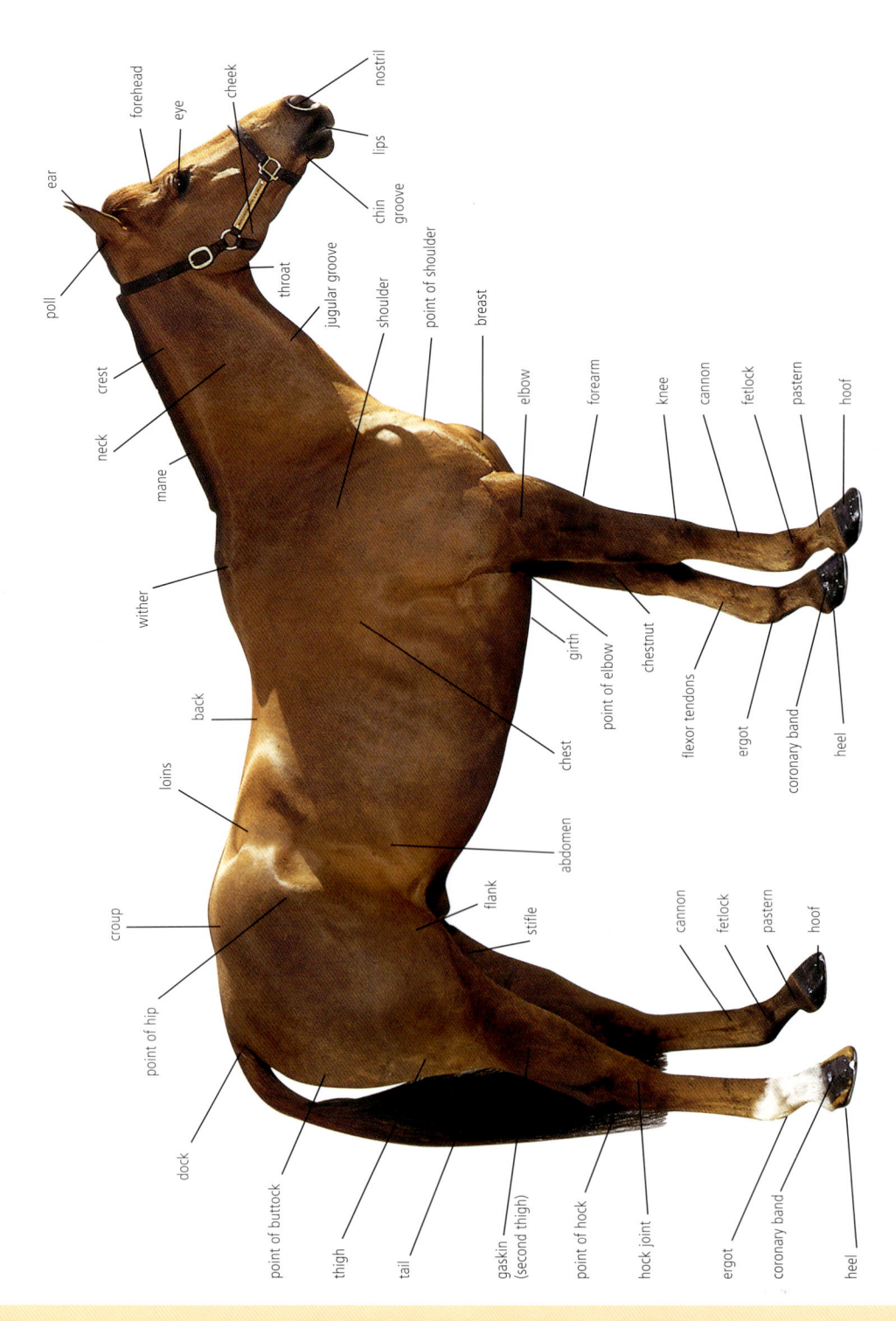

POINTS OF THE HORSE

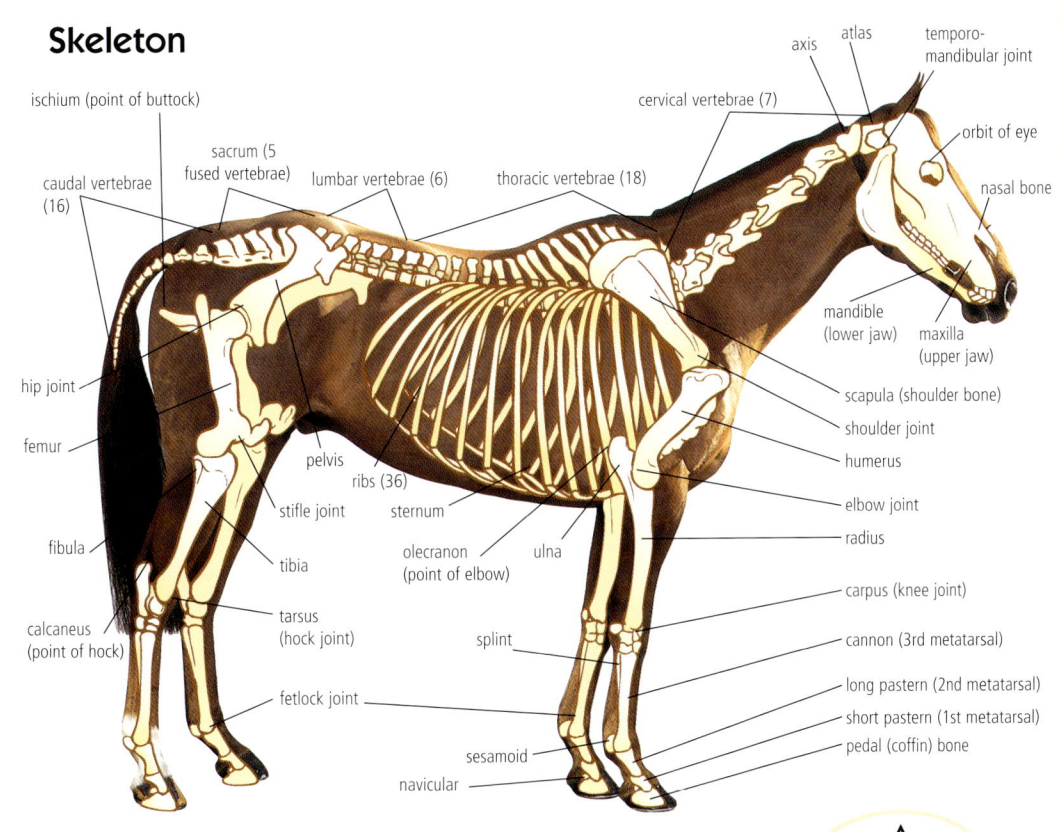

Skeleton

- ischium (point of buttock)
- caudal vertebrae (16)
- sacrum (5 fused vertebrae)
- lumbar vertebrae (6)
- thoracic vertebrae (18)
- cervical vertebrae (7)
- axis
- atlas
- temporo-mandibular joint
- orbit of eye
- nasal bone
- mandible (lower jaw)
- maxilla (upper jaw)
- scapula (shoulder bone)
- shoulder joint
- humerus
- elbow joint
- radius
- carpus (knee joint)
- cannon (3rd metatarsal)
- long pastern (2nd metatarsal)
- short pastern (1st metatarsal)
- pedal (coffin) bone
- hip joint
- femur
- pelvis
- ribs (36)
- stifle joint
- sternum
- tibia
- olecranon (point of elbow)
- ulna
- fibula
- calcaneus (point of hock)
- tarsus (hock joint)
- splint
- fetlock joint
- sesamoid
- navicular

Some definitions

- **Arteries** carry blood away from the heart. A cut artery pulses as it bleeds.
- **Bones** are a store for minerals and the marrow, which produces red blood cells.
- **Bursae** are sacs found near joints, such as the knee, or bony areas, such as the poll. They contain the lubricating synovial fluid.
- **Cartilage** is a smooth tough substance that allows smooth movement of the joints.
- **Collagen** is a fibrous tissue found in bones and tendons.
- **Joints** are found where ever two bones meet. Their ends are covered with cartilage and the most flexible joints, such as knees, hocks and fetlocks, are lubricated by synovial fluid produced by synovial membranes in the bursae.
- **Ligaments** attach bones to bones and consist of fibrous tissue in rigid bands.
- **Muscles** are made of fibrous tissue. They are usually connected to bones via tendons.
- **Tendons** attach muscles to bones and consist of collagen. They are not as flexible as muscles, which is why tendons are more usually strained than muscles. Flexor tendons flex the muscles, while extensor tendons extend them – so a leg is lifted by a flexor tendon and moved forward by an extensor tendon.
- **Veins** carry blood to the heart. A cut vein bleeds as a steady flow.

A horse's body:
- is 65% water
- contains up to 45 litres (79 pints) of blood
- produces up to 20kg (44lbs) of faeces and 9 litres (16 pints) of urine daily

Teeth and dental health

Some definitions

- **Adult teeth** These are large and yellow. It takes about six months from when they appear to when they are large enough to come into use.
- **Cup** The hole in the table (grinding surface), which gradually gets shallower as the teeth wear away with age. In the young horse its appearance is long and narrow on the table, with age it becomes oval and then triangular.
- **Dental star** A raised, brown-stained area on the table that consists of additional dentine, which grows to protect the nerves as the teeth are worn down.
- **Dentine** The hard substance that the teeth are mostly made from.
- **Galvayne's groove** A dark-coloured groove that begins to grow down the upper corner incisors at 9 or 10 years old.
- **Incisors** The row of teeth at the front of the mouth on both jaws.
- **Mark** When it has become very shallow, the cup is called the mark.
- **Milk teeth** These are baby teeth. They are small and white and are pointed where they emerge from the gum.
- **Molars** The large teeth at the back of the jaw, sometimes called cheek teeth.
- **Table** The grinding surface of the tooth.
- **Temporomandibular joint** The joint that joins the upper and lower jaws (see p.19). Poorly cared for teeth can inhibit the movement of this joint, which in turn may cause pain and hence behavioural problems.
- **Tushes** Small canine teeth mostly found in male horses, these grow near the corner incisors on both jaws and sometimes cause bitting problems.
- **Wolf teeth** Tiny teeth just in front of the first molars on both jaws. These often cause discomfort and are nearly always removed.

When to call the dentist

A dentist should visit your horse every six months. As well as these regular check ups, consider calling the dentist if your horse:

- starts being difficult to ride, or performs less well than usual;
- throws his head around or rears;
- develops a dislike of the bit or having the noseband done up;
- keeps putting his tongue over the bit;
- keeps putting his tongue out of his mouth when wearing a bridle;
- has any difficulty eating, including dropping food (quidding), bolting food, eating hay in preference to hard food, choking.

Common dental problems

- **Teething** – up to the age of 5 new teeth may cause discomfort and milk teeth may need to be removed when they are ready to be replaced by adult teeth.
- **Wolf teeth** – these need removal if they are uncomfortable or in the way of the bit.
- **Sharp edges** – the teeth grow continuously and are ground down by the horse eating. Uneven wear can produce sharp edges on the molars – on the outer edge of the upper jaw molars and the inner edge of the lower jaw molars.

Indicators of a painful mouth

- Discharge from eyes or nostrils
- Sensitive cheeks or lumps on jaw
- Excessive drooling
- Irregular movement of lower jaw
- Inability to shift lower jaw from side to side
- Bad breath
- Sores or bleeding on the lips, gums, palate
- Longer than normal particles in the manure
- Weight loss or poor condition despite good feeding

TEETH AND DENTAL HEALTH

Dental treatment

Usual treatment consists of the dentist using a selection of rasps to smooth off all the sharp edges on the teeth, including the molars at the back of the mouth – this is called floating. Plaque may also be removed from the tushes. A gag holds the horse's mouth open and he is held steady with a headcollar. The dentist will need a bucket of clean water and a clean well-lit stable or enclosed area. For removal of wolf teeth and more difficult or painful dentistry, such as dealing with abcesses, an anaesthetic may be used.

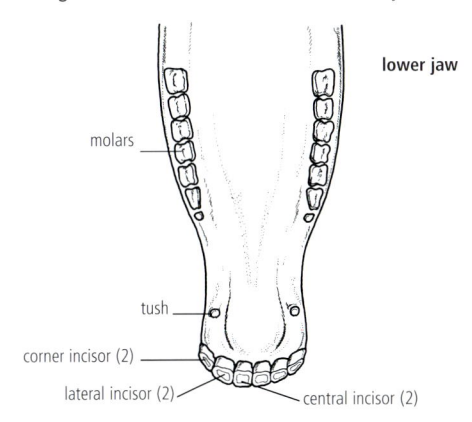

lower jaw
- molars
- tush
- corner incisor (2)
- lateral incisor (2)
- central incisor (2)

cross section through incisor — table (grinding surface)
- 4 years (cup)
- 8 years (mark)
- 12 years (dental star, triangular table)
- pulp cavity (nerves)

Ageing

A horse's age can be estimated by its incisors, particularly when young. With age the table alters from oval to triangular, the deep cup wears away, until it becomes the shallow 'mark', the dental star appears on the table, and the teeth stick out more at the front of the mouth.

Birthday
Horses are aged from 1 January, regardless of when they were born. If a horse's true sixth birthday is 12 April, he is said to be 'rising' 6 between 1 January and 12 April.

Telling the age of a horse

AGE	TEETH
1	Full set of milk incisors. The corners of the top and bottom set do not meet.
2½	Permanent central incisors appear.
3	Permanent central incisors are in use.
3½	Permanent lateral incisors appear.
4	Permanent lateral incisors are in use.
4½	Permanent corners appear.
5	All incisors in use. Tushes have appeared in geldings and some mares.
6	All incisors in use. Tables level and cups dark.
7	Central cups worn out, leaving paler 'mark'. The upper incisors may overlap the lower ones, producing a 'hook' on the back of the upper corner incisors.
8	Lateral cups worn out, leaving paler mark. Centrals have dental star. Hooks worn out.
9	Corner cups worn out, leaving paler mark. Laterals have dental star. Central tables become more triangular.
10	The lower end of Galvayne's groove appears on upper corner incisors, between 9 and 10 years old. On all incisors the marks are less distinct and the dental stars more distinct. Lateral tables become more triangular.
15	Galvayne's groove reaches about halfway down the upper corners.
20	Galvayne's groove reaches the table.
20+	Galvayne's groove's lower end emerges from the gum and gradually moves down until at 25 the upper end has emerged and is clear of the gum.

First aid for horses

First aid box

- Poultice (for use wet or dry)
- Antiseptic spray
- Antiseptic ointment
- Antiseptic cleaning liquid (for cleansing in dilution)
- Crepe bandages
- Self-adhesive bandages
- Cotton wool
- Epsom salts
- Gamgee
- Non-stick dressing
- Peroxide (20% vol)
- Salt
- Veterinary thermometer
- Tweezers
- Scissors
- Petroleum jelly
- Witch hazel
- Sticky back tape (such as silage tape, for fixing foot poultices)
- Eye ointment and eye wash
- Sunblock
- Stethoscope
- Clean bucket or bowl
- Hoof testers

Vital signs

Averages are given for horses at rest. Each horse is different; get to know yours.

Respiration around 12 breaths a minute at rest.

Pulse 36–42 a minute. Slightly more in younger horses.

Temperature 38.5°C (100.5°F). A temperature over 39.5°C (103°F) indicates a serious problem.

Measuring respiration

Stand behind the horse, slightly to one side.
Watch the rise and fall of the flanks.
Count the number of times they rise or fall (one breath is one rise, one fall) in one minute.
If the horse is worried or has just been running or exercising the rate will be higher.

Measuring pulse

The pulse is difficult to find so get some practise.
Try the top of the lower jaw near the throat, the cheek above the level of the eye, the inside fore-leg level with the knee joint.
Press your fingers gently against the pulse.
Count for 30 seconds then double the number.

Measuring temperature

Don't do this alone until you are experienced.
Shake the thermometer until it reads below 37°C (97°F).
Put a little petroleum jelly on the bulb end.
Stand to one side of the horse, raise the dock and insert the thermometer in the rectum, holding it tightly.
After 1–2 minutes withdraw thermometer and take the reading.
Clean and disinfect the thermometer.

digital pulse

Pulse points are indicated left. A digital pulse is only detectable when blood flow into the foot is constricted and it is taken as an indicator of feet problems such as laminitis.

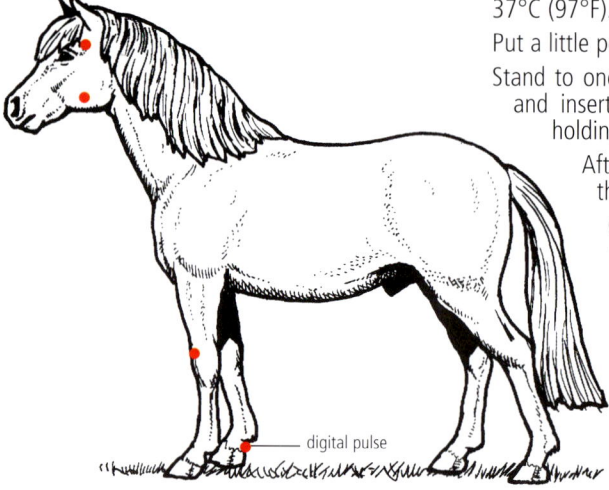

FIRST AID FOR HORSES

Treating your horse

Small cuts and bruises, mild lameness and minor eye infections may all be treated successfully by an experienced horse keeper. However, many horse ailments will require veterinary attention. Some of the most common problems are described here and the information given should help you to keep your horse comfortable and safe while you wait for the vet's arrival. Other problems are described on pp.28–31.

Mild eye infection
Symptoms
- More tears than usual
- Discharge from eye
- Puffiness in eyelid

Treatment
- Bathe with warm water
- Use a fly mask if the horse is being bothered by flies

Notes
- If symptoms persist or worsen call the vet who may suggest antibiotic eye drops
- If tears are rolling down the cheeks, the tear ducts could be blocked, in which case the vet will need to flush them out
- Where there are signs of damage and/or tenderness, call the vet; while awaiting their arrival, bathe with warm water then use a warm compress to ease the pain

Diarrhoea
Symptoms
- Loose droppings
- Horse becomes sickly
- Weight loss (if prolonged)

Treatment
Identify the cause and treat it accordingly:
- Stress or excitement – the diarrhoea will stop when the horse calms down
- Worm infestation – follow a sensible worming regime (see p.13)
- Recent move to rich pasture – limit the amount of time the horse spends in the pasture or reduce his grazing area
- Poisonous plants or any other suspected poisoning – call the vet immediately
- Bacterial infection, inflammation of the gut – need to be diagnosed and treated by the vet

Colic – abdominal pain

Colic appears more common in stable-kept horses, especially those recently stabled for long periods after being at pasture full time – for example, if they're brought in for box rest. Recent research suggests it may also be brought on by long journeys.

Symptoms – any or all
- Frantic rolling
- Biting or kicking at flanks
- Patchy sweating
- Pawing at ground
- Increased vital signs
- Lying down

Treatment
- Call the vet immediately
- Stable the horse
- Lay a deep bed as protection and to prevent him getting cast
- Keep him warm
- Allow him to drink if he wants to, but do not give any food
- Walk him gently (if recommended by vet) to discourage violent rolling
- Note droppings – loose, hard, or none at all
- If possible, note pulse, temperature and respiration
- Pain-killers, saline, lubricant may all be used by the vet. Twisted gut – a complication of colic – will require immediate surgery.

Choke – food stuck in the throat

Symptoms – any or all
- Coughing after being fed
- Horse very distressed and attempting to swallow
- Nasal discharge
- Increased vital signs
- Swelling visible in throat

Treatment
- Call the vet
- Gently massage the throat to encourage clearance of the blockage

Leg and feet problems

Abscess
Symptoms
- Extreme lameness
- Swelling in lower leg
- Heat in foot
- No obvious wounds or damage

Treatment
- The farrier or vet will use hoof testers to locate the site of the abscess and then dig a hole in the hoof to release the pus and enable the abscess to drain – after which the horse will instantly become much sounder
- Poulticing for 2 days, or until no more dark-coloured pus is seen on the poultice, is usually advised
- Antibiotics are rarely of use

Azoturia
Symptoms
- Hindquarters moving oddly due to swollen, painful muscles
- Profuse sweating and anxiety
- Dark-coloured urine

Treatment
- Call the vet
- Do not make the horse walk, keep him warm by putting a blanket over the quarters
- Prevent reoccurrence by balancing diet with workload (see p.34–37)

Thrush
Symptoms
- Blackness on sole of foot, especially around frog
- Dreadful smell
- Possibly lameness

Treatment
- Clean hooves and scrub away loose, crumbly material
- Disinfect with peroxide solution or purple spray
- Repeat twice daily
- Maintain good stable hygiene

Cuts
- Call a vet if: the wound is bleeding in spurts (a cut artery); the wound is very deep or lacerated, particularly if bone, tendon or other underlying tissue can be seen; clear liquid is visible (joint or tendon fluid); your horse hasn't got a current tetanus vaccination
- Small, shallow, clean cuts that are not bleeding heavily may be treated with antiseptic spray (or cream if the horse dislikes sprays)
- Deep cuts and larger wounds may require stitching (call the vet) and possibly antibiotics. Clean the wound (see below) and try to slow the bleeding; do not use antiseptics until advised by the vet

Cleaning wounds
- Wash your hands
- Get some clean cotton wool and a weak saline or antiseptic solution; with large leg wounds hosing with plain water may be more suitable
- Clean from the centre of the wound outwards
- Clean the surrounding skin
- Use a dressing to stop bleeding if necessary (see 'Fixing a bandage', below); bleeding may take some time to stop

Fixing a bandage
Bandages are usually used only on the legs as they will not stay in place elsewhere
- Place a non-stick dressing over the wound
- Wrap gamgee or other padding around the leg
- From above the wound, leaving an edge of padding visible and working downwards, wrap a bandage around the leg. Leave a margin of padding visible at the bottom, too. Make sure the pressure is even throughout the bandage
- If the dressing is covering a knee or hock, wrap the bandage in a figure of eight to avoid pressure on the joint

FIRST AID FOR HORSES

Laminitis/founder
Symptoms
- Lameness – severe or otherwise
- Heat in the feet
- Horse tries to stand on its heels, to relieve pain in the hoof

Treatment
- Call the vet
- Remove your horse from the source of the problem (see 'Causes of laminitis')
- Stable your horse on a deep bed
- Do not feed him until the vet has visited

Causes of laminitis
- Obesity
- Overfeeding/overeating
- Illness, such as Cushing's disease or hormonal imbalances
- Drugs, such as corticosteroids
- Concussion due to hard road work
- Cold weather
- Stress
- Secondary laminitis may develop when, for example, hindlegs are overworked because the forelegs have laminitis

Lameness

Most lameness (about 9 in 10 cases) occurs due to problems in the feet, such as abcesses, bruising, puncture wounds – which can all benefit from poulticing (see below) – and laminitis (left).

Even where the leg is swollen, the cause could be in the foot.

With slight lameness and no obvious swelling or injury, stable the horse for 24 hours and check again – calling the vet if he is still lame.

Intermittent lameness may indicate navicular disease (p.30) or pedal ostitis (p.30).

Tendon sprains, which may occur during turnout or exercise, are characterized by warmth and puffiness around the thickened tendon, as well as varying degrees of lameness – call the vet, cold hose the leg, bandage both it and its partner, then stable your horse until the vet arrives.

Applying a hot foot poultice
- Clean the foot
- Cut the poultice to size and shape
- Place it in warm water then gently squeeze to remove the excess
- Position the poultice over the sole of the hoof
- Keep it in place with self-adhesive bandage – wrap the bandage two or three times around the edge of the hoof first then gradually cover the poultice by bringing the bandage over the sole and around the hoof wall working up the hoof to the coronet, making sure you do not make it too tight when you reach the coronet
- Use a poultice boot or layers of sticky back tape to keep the whole thing in place (especially if the horse has to go back out into a field)

First aid for people

First aid box
Choose a clean waterproof container, mark it clearly and put it in an obvious place.
- A selection of individually wrapped adhesive dressings and plasters
- Sterile dressings
- Bandages – rolled and triangular
- Cotton wool – for padding only
- Wound cleasing wipes – alcohol-free
- Safety pins, scissors, tweezers
- Thermometer
- Torch, blanket, whistle

Vital signs
Respiration 12–16 breaths per minute in adults, 20–30 in babies and young children.
Pulse 60–80 per minute in adults, less in very fit people, more in babies.
Temperature 37°C (98.6°F).

Calling an ambulance
You will need to tell emergency services:
- ✔ Your exact location and clear directions to it
- ✔ What has happened and who is involved
- ✔ Your name and phone number

Important note
Riding is a risk sport but you can make it safer for yourself and others by being aware of the risks and how to deal with any incidents. Please go out and buy yourself a good first aid manual (authorized by a well-known first aid provider such as St John's Ambulance, St Andrew's Ambulance Association or the British Red Cross), get to know the book well, especially the basic first aid procedures, and then keep it readily to hand. Better still, go on a first aid course – you could save a life.

Shock
Symptoms
- Rapid pulse
- Cold skin, blue-tinged around the mouth
- Sweating
- Weakness
- Possibly leading to a weakened pulse and unconsciousness

Treatment
- Deal with any injuries
- Lie casualty down
- Raise their legs if possible
- Loosen tight clothing
- Keep them warm with a blanket
- Call an ambulance

Concussion
Symptoms
- Short-lived loss of consciousness
- Dizziness or nausea
- Memory loss
- Mild headache

Treatment
- If unconscious, follow the procedure outlined in 'Unconscious injured casualty' (opposite)
- If the casualty seems conscious, ensure they remain lying down, or sitting, until they can respond sensibly to questions and feel pain – a pinch
- If headache, nausea, vomiting, excessive drowsiness occur the casualty must be taken to hospital

Severe bleeding
Treatment
- Clear the wound of clothing
- Use a dressing and your hand to apply pressure to the wound
- Raise the wound – lie the casualty down
- Leaving the dressing in place, bandage the wound – not so tight that it restricts blood circulation
- Call an ambulance

FIRST AID FOR PEOPLE

Eye injury
Treatment
- The casualty should be taken to hospital lying down – call an ambulance if your car is unsuitable
- Tell them to keep their head and the uninjured eye still (this keeps the injured eye still too)
- Give them a clean dressing or other protection to put over the eye

Spinal injury
Symptoms
- Pain or tenderness in neck or back
- Limbs weak or unable to move
- Breathing difficulties
- Loss of bladder or bowel control

Treatment
- Keep the head and neck still and supported
- Call an ambulance

Broken bones
Symptoms
- Bruising and distortion
- Pain, especially when the limb is moved

Treatment
- Protect the break as far as possible
- Call an ambulance

Skull fracture
If there is severe bleeding from a head wound, the skull may also be damaged, this might be indicated by a loss of consciousness (even if only very short-lived). Clear liquid or watery blood leaking from an ear or the nose point to a severe head injury. Lie the casualty down and call an ambulance immediately.

Unconscious injured casualty
These points are a guide only, they are not a substitute for proper first-aid training. Where an unconscious person is not injured and not breathing the most likely cause is a heart attack – call an ambulance immediately.

- **Do not move the person** unless they are in danger where they are; don't remove their riding hat.

- **If the person is breathing**, put them in the recovery position (below left), unless you suspect a serious neck injury, and call an ambulance.

- **If the person is not breathing:**

Ensure that they can breathe by opening their airway – lie them on their back and tilt their head gently backwards (you may have to undo the chinstrap), open their mouth and carefully remove any obvious obstruction. Lift the chin.

- **If they don't immediately breathe on their own:**

Carry out rescue breaths – use one hand to pinch their nose closed, use the other to hold their chin, take a deep breath, place your mouth over their mouth, blow steadily until their chest rises (about 2 seconds), remove your mouth, check that their chest falls. Repeat this procedure once more, then check whether the casualty is breathing. If they are put them in the recovery position (below left) and call an ambulance.

If the casualty is still not breathing:

- Carry out CPR (cardiopulmonary resuscitation) and rescue breaths – kneeling beside them, place the heel of one hand on their breastbone, place your other hand on top and interlock the fingers, leaning over the casualty, with arms straight, press down vertically, depressing their chest by 4–5cm (1½–2in), release the pressure without removing your hands. Compress and release the chest 15 times quite quickly (at a rate of 100 compressions every 60 seconds). Now give two rescue breaths (as described above).

- If the casualty starts to breathe on their own, put them in the recovery position. If not, repeat the procedure described for one minute before calling for an ambulance. Continue with the procedure until help arrives.

Horse health

This is a brief guide to some of the problems that horses may experience. Unless you are absolutely sure what is wrong with your horse and are completely confident you can treat it yourself, you should always seek professional help.

Abscess Pus formed in the foot, causing extreme lameness, or under the skin in response to an infection. Antibiotics are sometimes used except in the cases of foot abscesses (see p.24) and **strangles**.

Arthritis (degenerative joint disease, DJD) This is inflammation in a joint or joints. Acute arthritis occurs due to a wound or infection; it causes heat and swelling and needs immediate treatment, including antibiotics and joint immoblization. Chronic arthritis develops more slowly and is often caused by repeated work-related stress on the joints; slower to develop, it produces stiffness and lameness. Although there is no cure, the symptoms can be relieved through gentle in-hand exercise, the use of anti-inflammatories (bute), and other drugs, including corticosteroids.

Aural plaques Crusty white scabs form inside the ear and the skin beneath is sensitive, pink and thickened. There is no completely successful treatment but bathing with anti-inflammatories will reduce the size of the plaques.

Azoturia See p.24.

Bog spavin See Bursal strains and injuries.

Botulism poisoning An often fatal poisoning, associated with eating infected food, such as soil-contaminated silage. Botulism causes muscle paralysis and respiratory failure. Symptoms appear about 4–5 days after infection: the horse has trouble eating and moving; he may stand with his head lowered.

Bruised sole A common cause of lameness, especially in the front feet. In white-footed horses bruising can be seen as a discoloured area: hoof-testers will also reveal sensitivity. Rest the horse, protecting the bruised foot, for 7–10 days. See also **Corns**.

Bursal strains and injuries (bursitis) Damage to the bursae (sacs) around bony areas, such as joints, causes over-production of the lubricating synovial fluid they contain, and this shows as soft swelling – called a bursal enlargement. Windgalls, bog spavins and thoroughpins are bursal strains. They are not very serious but may be initially painful. Treatment includes rest, cold hosing and massage. Capped hocks, elbows and knees are bursal injuries and are often painless, although it is sometimes advisable to drain the fluid from the area and apply a pressure bandage to prevent more building up.

Capped elbow/capped hock See Bursal strains and injuries.

Choke See p.23.

COPD (chronic obstructive pulmonary disease, heaves) A respiratory disease characterized by a hollow cough and reduced performance. It is caused by allergies, usually to mould spores in hay or straw, and possibly also pollen. A vet will treat symptoms then preventative measures, such as good stable hygiene, keeps COPD under control.

Colic See p.23.

Corns A cause of lameness, these are bruises at the heel of the foot and may result from infrequent shoeing or poor trimming. **Abscesses** may also develop in the area. Regular good quality farriery required. See also **Bruised sole**.

Curb A strain of the tendon at the back of the hock, indicated by a firm, perhaps warm swelling about 10cm (4in) below the point of hock, and possibly slight lameness in the early stages. A vet will treat inflammation; rest usually results in complete recovery.

Cushing's disease This is caused by a tumour on the pituitary gland, which affects hormone production. Symptoms include increased thirst and urination, the development of a long,

HORSE HEALTH

persistent curly coat, and a sway back and pot-belly. There is an increased proneness to laminitis and mouth ulcers, and healing of cuts becomes slower. No cure. A vet will suggest treatment to relieve symptoms and a good diet can help.

Dehydration Indicated by tight dry skin and depression. Dehydration can occur due to heavy sweating or as a result of diarrhoea. Water and electrolytes should stabilize the horse. If dehydration has not obviously been caused by workload call your vet immediately.

Endometritis An infection in mares (developed during foaling or because of an infected stallion) indicated by a persistent cloudy vulval discharge and a high temperature, possibly also laminitis and endotoxic shock. It also occurs due to a deformed vulva that allows air along with faecal contaminents to be drawn into the vagina (vulval aspiration); in this case a surgical procedure (Caslick's operation or Pouret's operation) is needed. See also **Endotoxaemia**.

Endotoxaemia An often fatal condition caused when bacteria from the intestines get into the rest of the horse's system, because of other problems such as colitis, twisted gut, concentrate overload. Indicators include depression, increased pulse rate, dehydration, colic-like symptoms, diarrhoea, excessive drinking.

Equine herpes virus (EHV) A series of viruses that cause respiratory, reproductive and neurological problems and spread mainly through the copious nasal discharge produced by infected animals. Incubation takes up to 10 days and horses may take 3 months to recover fully. Short-lived preventative vaccinations can be given; the viruses cannot be treated although some of the symptoms can be relieved with antibiotics and good nursing.

Equine infectious anaemia (EIA) A persistent virus initially causing fever, anaemia, body oedema and lethargy. Then recovery appears to take place but a few weeks later fluctuating periods of fever occur. Full recovery takes about a year but the horse has become a carrier. Coggins test diagnoses the disease; no treatment is available.

Equine influenza Most horses are vaccinated against equine flu, a serious respiratory disease (sometimes fatal in youngstock) causing high temperatures, clear nasal discharge and coughing. Incubation takes 3–4 days and recovery about 3 weeks. Treatment includes prolonged rest along with drug therapy. Recovered horses may be carriers.

Filled legs Horses kept stabled for long periods can suffer from poor circulation leading to swelling in the legs due to lymph escaping into surrounding tissues, rather than being circulated back up the legs. Increased turnout, a more roomy stable and stable bandages can help. It may degenerate into **lymphangitis**.

Head shaker A horse that shakes its head when ridden. Shaking is usually persistent; it may be mild or excessive. The cause may be nerve pain, and is often exacerbated by well known irritants such as pollen or dust. Full or partial facial nets are useful in many cases; drugs or surgery may help in others. Head shaking can also be caused by other physical problems, such as uncomfortable teeth.

Laminitis See p.25.

Locking patella This is where the stay mechanism that allows horses to doze while standing seizes up causing the leg to drag when the horse moves – it usually frees itself within minutes. It is a condition that often affects horses in poor health and disappears when they regain health. Surgery is sometimes required.

Lymphangitis Infection in the lymph vessels and tissues of the lower (usually hind) legs, causing hot and painful swelling and lameness. Liquid may ooze from the skin. Lymphangitis may be a complication of **mud fever**, **filled legs** or an untreated injury. Diuretics and anti-inflammatories are used to relieve it.

Mud fever (greasy heel) Inflammation and scabs on the heels and fetlocks caused by bacteria gaining entry through skin softened by being constantly wet and muddy. The pastern and fetlock may become swollen. Treatment includes cleansing the lower legs and using antibiotic ointment; barrier creams may help in prevention.

USEFUL INFORMATION

Navicular disease A degenerative disorder of the tiny navicular bone in the front feet. Symptoms include tripping and a gradual change of gait and onset of lameness. Drug therapies, surgery and remedial shoeing can relieve the symptoms.

Nose bleeds Bleeding from one or both nostrils after strenuous exercise. Bleeding may also be undetected as the blood goes down the trachea and is swallowed. Treatment is not always successful, although treatment of other respiratory problems can help, as can good stable hygiene.

Pedal ostitis Inflammation of the pedal bone of the front feet, leading to lameness. Anti-inflammatories and remedial shoeing can ease the symptoms.

Poisoning As horses are quite fussy eaters, they are very rarely poisoned. However, certain circumstances, such as food shortage, a huge fresh supply of a poisonous plant or it being present dried in forage, will sometimes lead them to eat what they would normally avoid. There are many forms of poisoning and few specific treatments (one example is dosing with thiamine to counteract bracken and mare's tail poisoning: these plants destroy this enzyme in the body), often the only recourse is to treat the symptoms and, unfortunately, the outcome is frequently death. (See also 'Poisonous plants', opposite and p.40.)

Rainscald (weather beat) Similar to **mud fever** except that it affects the body, rainscald is characterized by scabby areas on the back or neck, under which the skin is red and sore. In mild cases regular grooming will remove the problem, otherwise shampooing and antibiotic creams will be required. Antibiotics may be needed in severe cases.

Ringbone Slow-growing bony swelling on the pastern bones caused by concussion or injury. Where it restricts the action of the joints, it generally leads to long-term lameness; between the joints it often resolves after rest and treatment. Anti-inflammatory drugs and surgery may be required.

Ringworm Highly contagious disease (in people as well as animals) characterized by round, raised areas on the skin that grow and spread, bursting and becoming scabby. A vet will prescribe systemic antibiotics; antibiotic skin washes may also be used.

Sarcoid Tumour that can be likened to cancer, except that it affects only the skin. Sarcoids may be caused by viruses, but do not appear contagious. A damaged sarcoid can become aggressive and start growing and spreading more quickly, which makes biopsies or half-hearted attempts at treatment a risk. If the sarcoid is 'quiet' and not in a place where it might cause problems (such as under the saddle), it may be best left alone. If treatment is decided upon, it must be carried out under a vet's guidance, with careful monitoring at all stages. Treatment may include surgical removal or freezing of the sarcoid, radiation treatment or the use of highly toxic ointments.

Sand cracks See p.45.

Seedy toe See p.45.

Sesamoiditis Disease in or damage to the sesamoid bones, which causes pain and swelling at the back of the fetlock joint and lameness. A vet will prescribe long rest (up to a year) and anti-inflammatory drugs.

Spavin Causing lameness in the hindlegs, this is a form of **arthritis** affecting the small bones in the hock.

Splint A hard swelling between the cannon and splint bones, often on the front legs, in young horses. As they form, they may be warm and cause lameness, but mature splints are cold and rarely cause trouble. Rest and anti-inflammatory treatment usually recommended.

Strangles A highly contagious infection of the upper respiratory tract causing raised temperature, nasal discharge, loss of appetite and swelling around the jaw due to **abscesses** in the throat. Infected horses must be isolated for at least 3 weeks. Hot poulticing helps the abscesses to drain. A vet will confirm the disease and recommend suitable treatment. Antibiotics are rarely used.

Stringhalt Horses affected by stringhalt have an odd hindleg action, lifting the legs over-high

HORSE HEALTH

and slamming them down hard. In some countries, dandelion poisoning may be implicated. Muscle relaxants can be an effective treatment; surgery is sometimes used.

Sweet itch An allergic reaction to midge saliva, sweet itch causes the affected horse to rub itself raw on the mane and/or tail. Barrier rugs stop the midges getting to the skin and their use can be combined with fly repellents. Corticosteroids can be used, but have side effects, including increased proneness to laminitis.

Thoroughpin See Bursal strains and injuries.

Thrush See p.24.

Uveitis (moonblindness) This disease affects the inside and outside of the eye, as well as the surrounding tissues, and is extremely painful for the horse. The pupil constricts and the eye becomes very sensitive to light. Copious tears are produced, and the eyelids, which are inflamed, tend to be fast-closed. The cause may be bacteria or worm larvae; treatment includes antibiotics, corticosteroids and atropine. The problem tends to reoccur and eventually leads to blindness.

Urticaria (hives) Lumps appearing on the skin in association with swollen facial features and legs are a sign of an allergic reaction, usually to a change of diet or an insect bite. Antihistamine or corticosteroids are administered by the vet to relieve the symptoms.

Warts Small warts appear on the thin-skinned areas of a horse, such as the nostrils or eyelids. They usually occur in young horses and will grow, changing from grey to reddish, then drop off. Although they can be removed by the vet, they will disappear of their own accord after 3–4 months.

Windgalls See Bursal strains and injuries.

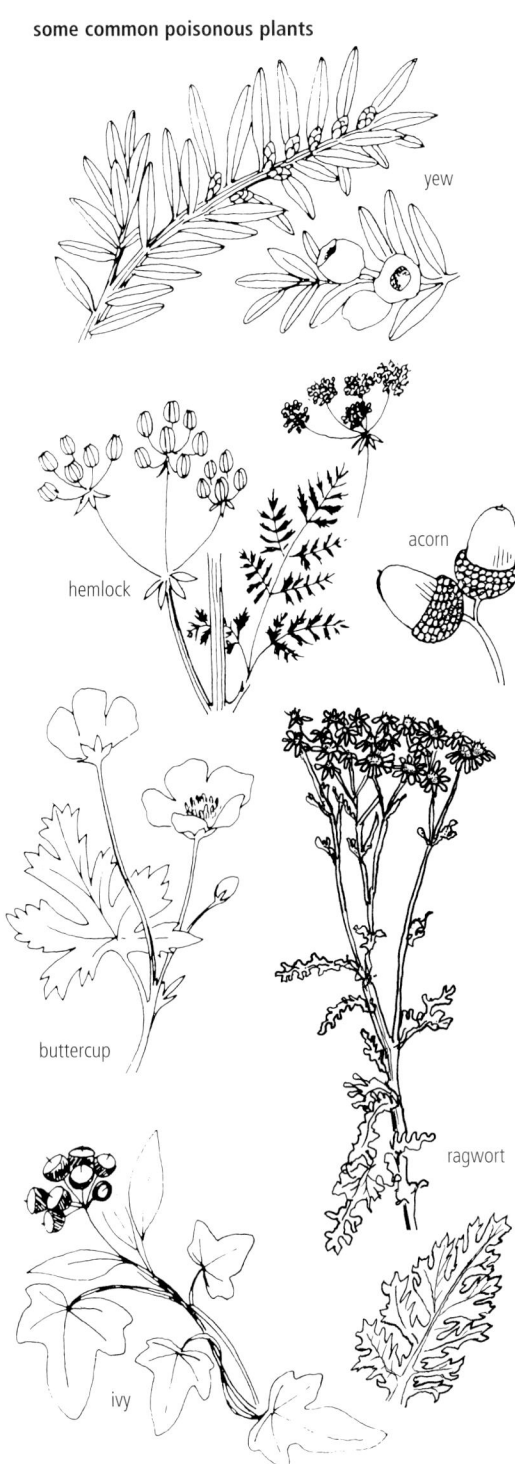

some common poisonous plants

yew

hemlock

acorn

buttercup

ragwort

ivy

Road safety

Advice to riders
- Wear a hard hat when riding on the road; in Britain children under 14 years old must wear one, otherwise their parents may face prosecution (see p.7).
- Wear high visibility gear (tabards or leg and arm bands) even in summer, when shadows or the sun can prevent drivers seeing you.
- Be courteous to drivers and other road users, even if they are not courteous in return – next time they might be.
- Get third party insurance so if you are involved in an accident you are covered for any damage you or your horse do.
- Learn the Highway Code/Vehicle Code and, in Britain, take your BHS Riding and Safety Road Test (see 'By law', below right).
- If you or your horse are inexperienced or nervous of traffic, ride on the road only during calm periods and always with a calm escort.
- Never take risks – if your horse is scared of something on the road, wait until all is clear before passing.
- If safety dictates, ride a little out from the curb to be more visible or to prevent cars passing where it might be dangerous.
- Don't ride on icy roads.

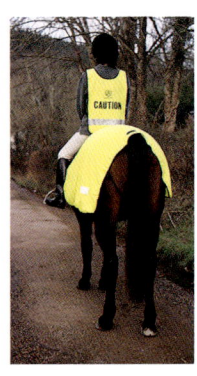

Advice to drivers
- Give horses a wide berth and pass slowly – remember, they are not like cars, they can leap sideways into the road if something on the roadside startles them.
- Drive slowly on country roads and lanes – horses, walkers and other slow traffic might be just around the corner.
- If you are behind a horse and a vehicle is approaching in the opposite direction, wait for it to pass before passing the horse.

Roadcraft
- Ask a driver to slow down by stretching your arm out, palm down, then raising and lowering your arm.
- Ask a driver to stop by raising your hand, palm out towards the driver.
- Use your arm to indicate clearly which way you are turning.
- Before making any manoeuvre Look, Listen, Observe, Look Again – this is the Life-saver Look.
- Whatever way you are turning, stay by the kerb until the road is clear.
- On roundabouts keep by the kerb until you reach your turning.
- Obey road signs and traffic lights.

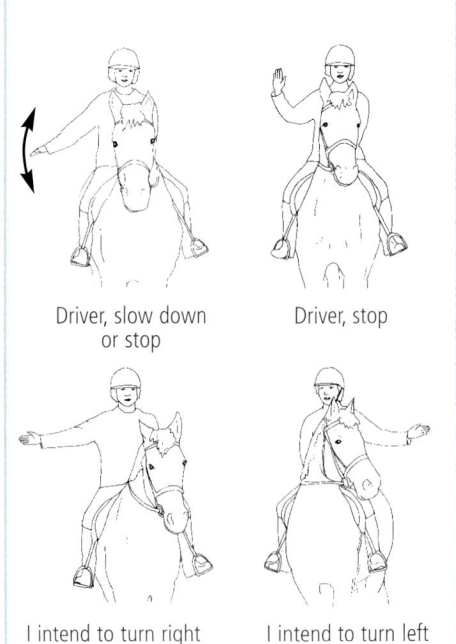

Driver, slow down or stop

Driver, stop

I intend to turn right

I intend to turn left

By law
- You must not ride on a pedestrian path or pavement.
- In the UK and parts of the USA, you must wear a hard hat if you are under 14.

Trailers and horse boxes

Before loading ask yourself*:
Is the trailer or lorry appropriate for my horse?
- ✔ Check capacity (see 'MAM').
- ✔ Check internal size – there should be space for your horse to stand easily without restriction, and allow at least 20cm (8in) above his natural head height.
- ✔ Make sure it's clean and well ventilated.
- ✔ Check the floor is non-slip and any partitions are fitted properly.
- ✔ Is it safe (see also Insurance)?
- ✔ Check the flooring, the condition of the towbar, the state of the wheels, the lights.

Is my vehicle appropriate for towing?
- ✔ It must be capable of towing the combined weight of the trailer and its maximum load (indicated in the handbook, or check with the manufacturer).
- ✔ The combined weight of the trailer and its maximum load should be less than 85% of the actual weight of the towing vehicle.
- ✔ 4-wheel drives are best for towing trailers as they cope better with hills and off-road driving.
- ✔ Check oil, water, tyre pressure; keep the vehicle well maintained.
- ✔ Carry a fire extinguisher, a breakdown triangle and a torch.

Am I safe?
- ✔ In Britain, if you passed your driving test after 1st January 1997 your MAM is 3,500kg – usually easily exceeded by a tow vehicle, let alone the trailer. Take an additional driving test to be legal.
- ✔ If you passed your driving test before 1st January 1997 but are inexperienced at towing, you owe it to your horse to take an additional driving test.
- ✔ If you're a bit rusty, practise reversing and pulling away with the trailer empty.
- ✔ Take a mobile phone – remember your breakdown assistance numbers and card – and something fluorescent to wear in the event of a breakdown. It is preferable to take someone with you to help if necessary.
- ✔ Make sure you know how to change a tyre.

(*Obviously, some of these points only relate to trailers.)

MAM/MGW
Maximum authorized mass, or maximum gross weight, indicates the loading capacity of a trailer or lorry. The MAM is usually indicated on a manufacturer's plate on the vehicle, often on the towbar on trailers.

Towing Ability Test
In Britain you can find out where to do a towing ability test by contacting an approved driving instructor. Or, contact trailer manufacturers who will be able to help.

Insurance
Your insurance will be invalidated if:
- ✘ your vehicle is not appropriate for pulling your trailer.
- ✘ you are not licensed to tow a trailer.
- ✘ you exceed the MAM.

Before transporting someone else's horse ensure your insurance covers you.

Long journeys
- ✔ Provide a deep bed.
- ✔ Feed and water at least every 6–8 hours.
- ✔ Allow space for foals and young horses to lie down on journeys of more than 12 hours.
- ✔ Plan ahead for stops where horses can be unloaded and rested with shelter.

Know the law
The Equine Law and Horsemanship Safety website (www.utexas.edu/dawson), set up and maintained by the University of Texas and the AAHS (American Association for Horsemanship Safety), details laws affecting horses and horse riders in the USA, along with lots of other useful information.

ROAD SAFETY 33

Feeding your horse

Feeding facts
- Horses like to eat for 16–20 hours a day.
- A grass-kept horse can eat 2–3kg (4–6½lbs) of grass an hour, which means up to 60kg (132¼lb) a day.
- A horse can eat about 2.5% of its total weight daily – this is its total appetite.
- Sufficient roughage is vital in maintaining a healthy horse; balance between roughage and concentrate is also vital (see 'How much forage?' p.37).
- Good quality concentrate mixes (sweet feeds) are nutritionally balanced – choose the correct energy level and feed the amounts suggested, and you shouldn't need to feed supplements; if you feed less than the recommended levels (see 'Feed Chart', p.36), consider including a broad spectrum supplement.
- Always alter a horse's diet gradually to give the bacteria in his gut time to adjust.
- A horse requires up to 55 litres (12 gallons) of water a day.
- Salt should always be available to your horse – usually in the form of a salt lick, but don't put it near the water trough.
- Overfeeding concentrates will exaggerate a horse's natural behaviour but cannot change his character.

Some definitions
- **Lignin** – woody fibres in plant material, these cannot be digested by the horse.
- **Cellulose** – slightly less woody than lignin, these can be digested.
- **Cereal concentrates** – grains such as oats, wheat, barley, maize, corn.
- **Non-cereal concentrates** – sugar beet, alfalfa, beans, peas, linseed, soya beans.
- **MJ** (**m**ega**j**oule) – a unit of energy equivalent to 240 calories.
- **DE** (**d**igestible **e**nergy) – the energy the horse can actually get out of the food.
- **Electrolytes** – also called tissue salts, these are sodium, potassium, chlorine and they regulate body fluids.

Nutrition
These ingredients make up a horse's diet:
- ✦**Carbohydrate**, about two-thirds of the diet, is the main provider of heat and energy.
- ✦**Protein**, about one sixth of the diet, is for body tissue repair and muscle development.
- ✦**Oil/fat**, about one sixth of the horse's diet, provides more heat and energy, but more slowly, than the same amount of carbohydrate (it has 35mj de/kg); however, it is fed in smaller quantities. It conditions skin, hair, horn.
- ✦**Fibre** is found in the food that provides protein and carbohydrate and is essential for a healthy gut.
- ✦**Vitamins and minerals** are required in very small quantities, overdoses can be as dangerous as deficiencies.
- ✦**Water** is essential for all life.

What does your horse weigh?
The easiest way to find out what your horse weighs is with a weigh tape. These are cheap, widely available, simple to use and reasonably accurate. Otherwise, you can estimate using the following formula:

$$\text{weight (kgs)} = \frac{\text{girth} \times \text{length} \times \text{length}}{11{,}000}$$

(Note: girth is the circumference of the horse just behind its front legs, length is from point of shoulder to point of buttocks. Remember to use centimetres.)

Table of weights
This table gives only a very rough guide to weight as so much depends on the horse's build – even if they are both the same height, a slight thoroughbred is likely to be somewhat lighter than a heavily built cob.

height	weight
10hh	to 190kg (419lb)
11hh	to 200kg (440lb)
12hh	to 300kg (660lb)
13hh	to 350kg (772lb)
14hh	to 400kg (882lb)
14.2hh	to 450kg (992lb)
15–15.2hh	to 500kg (1,102lb)
16–16.2hh	to 550kg (1,212lb)
17–17.2hh	to 600kg (1,323lb)

FEEDING YOUR HORSE

Vitamins and minerals
The vitamins a horse requires are:

Vitamin A for eyesight, mucous membranes and skin health. Vitamin A is readily available in good summer pasture. Feed carrots and oil in winter to boost vitamin A levels.

Vitamin B-group necessary for red blood cell formation and a balanced metabolism. Gut activity from a high fibre diet produces vitamin B. Horses in hard work may benefit from a supplement.

Vitamin C for tissue health and to aid disease defence mechanisms. It is usually produced in sufficient quantities by a healthy digestive system, although stressed horses may benefit from a supplement.

Vitamin D for bone formation. Sunlight enables a horse to produce its own vitamin D. Feed oil in winter to overcome deficiencies caused by lack of sunlight.

Vitamin E for a healthy immune system and red blood cell production. It is usually freely available in good pastures and from concentrates.

Vitamin K is stored by the horse and usually freely available in good pasture.

The major minerals a horse requires are:

Calcium (Ca), **phosphorus (P)** with vitamin D for bone maintenance.

Magnesium (Mg) for bone structure and to activate enzymes.

Sulphur (S) for the production of enzymes, hormones and amino acids.

Sodium (Na), **potassium (K)**, **chloride (Cl)** for regulating body fluids.
Potassium is found in forage, the other major minerals are usually provided in sufficient quantities in good quality feeds.

The trace minerals a horse requires are:

Copper (Cu), **iron (Fe)** to aid blood formation

Selenium (Se) with vitamin E for muscle strength.

Cobalt (Co), **iodine (I)**, **manganese (Mn)**, **zinc (Zn)**.
Trace minerals are all usually provided in sufficient quanties in good quality feeds.

Does your horse need supplements?

- How old is your horse? Older horses are less able to absorb vitamins and minerals; youngsters may need additional vitamins or minerals, as might mares in foal.
- How is he kept? Stabled horses are more likely to be deficient than grass-kept ones.
- How much work does he get? A high-performance horse will require more vitamins and minerals than a horse kept for light hacking.
- How good is the pasture? Some soils and, therefore, the grasses growing on them are deficient in minerals such as potassium, iron, zinc, sulphur, selenium.
- How good is your forage? Hay and haylage made in areas where the soil is deficient may also be deficient.

A label on a typical mixed concentrate feed

An analysis of the nutrients:
In the European Union, bags of concentrated feed (sweet feed) must indicate the dry weight percentage they contain of each nutrient, except carbohydrate but including the types and amounts of vitamins and minerals. Ash is any inorganic material other than protein, oil and carbohydrate; this indicates the percentage of vitamins and minerals:

Oil 4.0%
Protein 12.0%
Fibre 11.0%
Ash 7.5%
Moisture 14.4%
Vitamin A 14025 i.u./kg; Vitamin D3 1500 i.u./kg; Vitamin E 207 i.u./kg; Selenium 0.43 mg/kg; Copper 44 mg/kg

A best before date:
If you feed after this date the quality and quantity of vitamins and minerals present may have declined.

A list of ingredients:
The ingredients are listed in descending order by weight; this means that feed is made up of mostly the first few items; the last few items (usually the vitamins and minerals) are only present in tiny quantities.

Feed Chart

This chart shows the total number of megajoules (mj) of digestible energy (de) required by horses of various sizes in various types of work. As it is vital to feed the correct ratio of forage to concentrate (see 'How much forage?', p.37), the chart also shows the number of megajoules required from forage and from concentrate, assuming that the forage contains 7mj de/kg (reasonable quality hay) and the concentrate contains 12mj de/kg (an average concentrate/sweet feed mix). Beneath these figures are shown the weight required of each, so, for example, a 200kg horse in light work requires 4.5kg of forage and 850gm of concentrate a day. The chart will, therefore, give a rough idea of how much you should feed your horse and in what proportion; it should also be fairly easy to work out how much more or less you should feed as his weight or work varies. Before working out a ration, read the notes below.

Horse weight (kg)	Light work total mj = forage + concentrate	Medium work total mj = forage + concentrate	Hard work total mj = forage + concentrate
200	42 = 32 + 10 = 4.5 + 0.85	50 = 25 + 25 = 3.5 + 2	58 = 15 + 43 = 2 + 3.5
250	48 = 36 + 12 = 5 + 1	58 = 29 + 29 = 4 + 2.5	68 = 17 + 51 = 2.5 + 4.25
300	54 = 41 + 13 = 6 + 1.1	66 = 33 + 33 = 4.75 + 2.75	78 = 20 + 58 = 3 + 5
350	60 = 45 + 15 = 6.5 + 1.25	74 = 37 + 37 = 5.25 + 3	88 = 22 + 66 = 3 + 5.5
400	66 = 50 + 16 = 7 + 1.3	82 = 41 + 41 = 6 + 3.5	98 = 25 + 73 = 3.5 + 6
450	72 = 54 + 18 = 7.75 + 1.5	90 = 45 + 45 = 6.5 + 3.75	108 = 27 + 81 = 4 + 6.75
500	78 = 59 + 19 = 8.5 + 1.6	98 = 49 + 49 = 7 + 4	118 = 30 + 88 = 4.25 + 7.25
550	84 = 63 + 21 = 9 + 1.75	106 = 53 + 53 = 7.5 + 4.5	128 = 32 + 96 = 4.5 + 8
600	90 = 68 + 22 = 9.75 + 1.8	114 = 57 + 57 = 8 + 4.75	138 = 34 + 103 = 5 + 8.5
	1 hour walking daily	walking, trotting and some cantering daily	1-day event/training or competing

Notes:
- This chart is a guide only – monitor your horse's weight, work level and performance and be prepared to adjust how much you feed as necessary.
- All horses are different, some will do very well on very little, while others need more to stay in condition.
- Remember that a horse at grass will eat almost continually – grass contains around 2.5mj de/kg (see 'Feeding facts', p.34). Take this into account in your calculations.
- The chart assumes that the horse is the correct weight to begin with. If weight loss or weight gain is required, feed slightly more or slightly less, remembering that a horse has a finite appetite (see 'Feeding facts', p.34).

Relative weights:
A slice of hay = 2kg
A scoop of cubes = 1.5kg
A scoop of concentrate (sweet feed) = 1kg
A double handful of chaff = 250g
A glop of oil = 100g

FEEDING YOUR HORSE

Ingredients in concentrate mixes (sweet feeds)

These are some of the ingredients used in concentrates. None should be fed in isolation.

Oats – bruised, crushed or rolled; reasonably high in fibre compared to other cereals; have a reputation for making horses fizzy, perhaps because they are easily digested, making the energy they contain quickly available. 11–12mj de/kg.

Barley – bruised, crushed or rolled; cannot be fed whole unless boiled. 12–13mj de/kg.

Wheat – usually micronized or as bran; high fibre content. 12–13mj de/kg.

Maize – usually flaked or otherwise processed; higher energy content than oats or barley, but processing reduces this. 14–15mj de/kg.

Sugar beet – high energy source, but slow-release; rich in salt. If fed separately, it is best to feed the unmolassed variety; molasses encourage a horse to eat much faster and the molassed type may be 40% molasses. 10.5mj de/kg.

Soya beans – cooked or processed; very protein rich, even as soya bean meal, which has had the oil extracted. 13–15mj de/kg.

Peas – cooked or processed; very protein rich. 14mj de/kg.

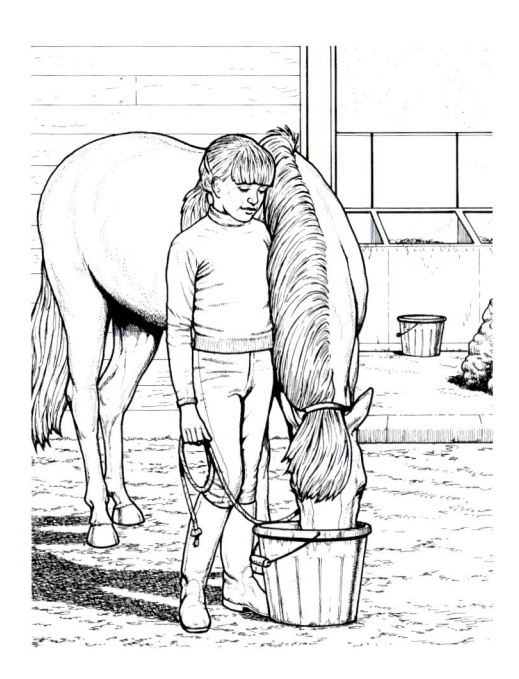

Forage

- **Hay** – grass cut and dried when mature and stalky so much of the nutrient content is trapped in the stalks as indigestible lignin. Meadow hay contains a variety of grasses – rye grass, cocksfoot, timothy – along with some clover and herbs. Seed hay is made from a specially grown grass crop, usually rye grass. Seed hay is more nutritious than meadow hay, lighter in colour and feels harder when you touch it. Soak all hay before feeding it. 7–9mj de/kg depending on quality.

- **Haylage** – grass cut and partially dried then vacuum-packed so it ferments. Often highly nutritious, but eaten almost twice as quickly as hay – 1kg (2lb) of haylage takes about 12 minutes to eat while 1kg (2lb) of hay takes about 20 minutes. Also, because haylage contains more water than hay, more of it by weight, must be fed. About 6mj de/kg.

- **Silage** – pickled grass, best not fed to horses as there is the risk of botulism (see p.28) and contamination from soil. High protein content.

- **Oat straw** – the stalky by-product of harvesting oats. Provides additional roughage; most of its nutrients are trapped in the lignin. Wheat and barley straws are not really suitable for feeding. Oat straw 8mj de/kg; barley staw 7mj de/kg.

- **Grass** – this is sold dried for horses with respiratory problems and other dietary needs. It is very nutritious but also expensive. Good mixed with cereal feed to balance out deficiencies. About 2.5mj de/kg growing, 10mj de/kg when dried.

- **Alfalfa/lucerne** – dried or in a molassed chaff form. Good mixed with cereal feed to balance out deficiencies. It is high in protein, calcium, vitamins and minerals. About 9mj de/kg.

How much forage?

These figures are by weight for mature horses.

Resting – wholly forage

Light to medium work – ¾ forage ¼ concentrate

Medium – ½ forage ½ concentrate

Hard work – up to ¼ forage ¾ concentrate

Perfect pastures

Some definitions
- **Harrowing** – removal of matted dead grass by means of a chain harrow pulled by a 4-wheel drive, ATV or tractor. Done in late winter or early spring it will also improve poached areas, especially if the field is rolled afterwards.
- **Leaching** – an effect similar to rinsing. Many fertilizers are leached out of the soil by rain, meaning they end up in local waterways and are no longer available to grasses and other plants.
- **pH** – the measurement of acidity and alkalinity. pH 7 is neutral, lower than that is acid (eg pH 6), higher is alkaline (eg pH 7.5). Soil pH affects grass growth (see 'Know your soil').
- **Poaching** – muddy rutted conditions that develop where drainage is poor or where animals congregate.
- **Tillering** – the formation of small shoots at the base of the grass, enabling it to spread.
- **Topping** – mowing grass at a high setting to remove tall and/or rank growth and weeds.

Paddock care
- Ideally, divide land into 3 paddocks: one being used, one being renovated (weed-killing, reseeding, fertilizing, harrowing), one growing.
- Consider improving drainage. Good drainage vastly improves pasture and is well worth the initial expense.
- Where complete renovation is required, use cattle to eat the pasture bare, harrow, seed and roll, then graze lightly with sheep. After this rest until there is even growth throughout the paddock.

Weedkilling
Consider spot weedkilling or digging up nuisance plants, such as docks and thistles, rather than wholesale spraying, which is less environmentally friendly and will kill off herbs and other plants that horses really enjoy eating (see 'Herbs', p.40).

Assessing pasture
- Boundaries – are they safe (see 'Considering boundaries', below right)?
- Clean – is the field mostly clear of manure and rough patches of grass?
- Convenient – is it easy to access the field, are approaches easy, is parking safe?
- Gates – are they secure, do they open into the field (safer)? Is allowance made for poaching in winter? Mesh or stone topping reduce poaching.
- Grass quality – is there plenty of grass, few weeds, no poisonous plants? Indicators of poor grazing include horsetails, thistles, bracken, docks, rushes and sedges, damp areas.
- Shelter – is there shelter (even if only trees or banks), is it enough for all the horses to use, is it sheltered from prevailing weather, is it sufficiently well-drained to avoid poaching?
- Size – is there at least 0.4ha (1 acre) available for each horse, with the possibility of rotation to rest the paddocks?
- Suitability – is it a good pasture for your horse? Does he need restricted grazing or particularly good fencing? Can this be arranged?
- Water – is the supply clean, constant and within easy reach? Are the troughs safe for horses – no sharp corners?

Horse manure
- ✔ Pick up daily or every other day to maximize areas for eating.
- ✔ Spread on fields (if necessary) when well rotted – preferably at least 1 year.
- ✔ Spread in autumn on paddocks due for winter resting and spring on the winter paddocks.
- ✔ Keep horses off for 6 months to prevent parasite infestation (see 'Worms and worming', p.40).
- ✔ Harrowing instead of poo-picking simply spreads the worm eggs but can be done if the field is then well rested (eg for hay) or cross grazed (1 cow/6 sheep an 0.4ha/acre).

PERFECT PASTURES

Know your soil
Sandy soil
- Good drainage, not so likely to poach.
- Remains good for riding on year-round.
- Warms up quickly in spring, so grass growth starts early.
- Grows poor grass, particularly in summer.
- Needs regular fertilization.
- Benefits from addition of organic matter, such as farmyard manure.

Clay soil
- Cold, so grass growth is slow to start in spring.
- Grows good grass.
- Gets very hard in summer, deep and muddy in winter.
- Only suitable for riding on in spring/autumn.
- Likely to be reasonably fertile.
- Benefits from drainage work.

Acid/alkaline?
- Ideal pH is 6.5. Simple soil testing kits are sold at garden centres – test several sample areas. Some fertilizer companies will carry out soil analysis, which will also tell you whether other nutrients are low (see 'Inorganic fertilizers').
- Improve alkaline soil by adding farmyard manure, which is acid, in autumn or winter. Keep horses off for at least two months.
- Improve acid soil by liming (basic slag will also provide phosphates, see 'Inorganic fertilizers') – up to 5,000kg per ha (2 tons per acre) in autumn or winter (every 5–8 years). Keep horses off until rain has washed it in.
- Any improvements are short-lived so regular testing and improving is required.

Using fertilizers
Inorganic fertilizers
These include nitrogen, phosphorus (phosphate) and potassium (potash), all necessary for plant growth and health.

Phosphorus
- Encourages clover, which improves nitrogen content (see 'Pasture plants', p.41)
- Use with care as it can upset horse's calcium:phosphorus balance (see p.35)
- Where required, apply it every 2–3 years

Potassium
- Likely to be deficient in lime-rich soils
- Not easily leached out by rain
- Annual dressing is recommended except where soils are rich in potash

Nitrogen
- Is likely to be naturally present in reasonable quantities in good pasture or pastures containing clover
- Easily leached out by rain

Organic fertilizer
- This is farmyard manure, preferably from straw-bedded cattle that are not being fed with hormones and other nutrients that are toxic to horses.
- Contains phosphate which dissolves slowly into the soil, providing a steady supply
- Contains potash in a similar form to that found in inorganic fertilizer
- Contains nitrogen in a number of forms, some of which break down slowly for plant use
- Spread in autumn/winter or before a field is left to grow hay

Considering boundaries
- **Fences** are best positioned following contours rather than up and down them.
- **Fence off hazards** such as rabbit holes, oak trees (so horses don't eat acorns), stagnant pools.
- **Post and rail** is best (rails at 1.2m and 30–45cm/4ft and 12–18in from the ground). Posts should be on the outside of the fence, away from the horses and should end at the top rail.
- **Post and plain wire** with a top timber rail and taut wire is acceptable; the lowest strand 30–45cm (12–18in) from the ground.
- **Wire mesh** (sheep, pig or stock wire) needs to be used carefully to avoid horses getting their feet caught in it.
- **Hedges and banks** should be well maintained and without poisonous plants. They provide good shelter.
- **Electric fencing** is ideal for temporary enclosures – white tape or rope is most visible for horses and people. A single strand is usually adequate.
- Never use **barbed wire**. If barbed wire is already present, remove it or cordon it off with electric fencing.

USEFUL INFORMATION

Poisonous plants

These are key poisonous plants, but many others are also dangerous. Luckily, horses rarely eat poisonous plants unless there is nothing else to graze on. Therefore, ensure good grazing and supplemental feeding if necessary. Often these plants are more palatable when dry, so make sure they are not in your hay (see p.31).

- ✘ Black nightshade (*Solanum nigrum*)
- ✘ Bracken (*Pteridium*)
- ✘ Buttercup (*Ranunculus*)
- ✘ Foxglove (*Digitalis*)
- ✘ Horsetails (*Equisetum*)
- ✘ Laurel (*Laurus*)
- ✘ Deadly nightshade (*Atropa belladonna*)
- ✘ Privet (*Ligustrum*)
- ✘ Ragwort (*Senecio*) – the most common cause of livestock poisoning in the UK
- ✘ Rhododendron (*Rhododendron ponticum*)
- ✘ Yew (*Taxus*)

Worms and worming

- ✦ A typical lifecycle – eggs are passed out in dung, the larvae hatch and develop. After about a week they distribute themselves in water present on the surface of grass, the horse ingests them and they develop into the adult (egg-laying) worm in the horse's digestive system.
- ✦ Larvae are discouraged by dry pastures and low temperatures.
- ✦ Avoid grazing grass too low as most larvae are found close to the ground.
- ✦ Horses develop some resistance through exposure to low worm infestations, but no horse can cope with a large burden.
- ✦ Worm all horses in the yard at the same time with the same wormer.
- ✦ Worm new arrivals and keep them in for at least 48 hours before turning them out with other horses.
- ✦ Dose for worms 48 hours before moving horses to a clean pasture.
- ✦ For more worming guidelines, see 'A worming calendar', p.13.

A new pasture
Considerations for new pastures:

- ✦ Difficult and expensive – best done by contractors.
- ✦ Timing is weather dependent – spring and autumn are best.
- ✦ It needs about a year to settle before horses can be grazed on it.
- ✦ Choose a seed mix specially for horses, including plenty of late-flowering grasses.
- ✦ Incorporate some clover (not more than 30% coverage or the pasture becomes too rich).
- ✦ Consider some fescues for strength if horses are to be exercised in the field.
- ✦ Include some wild herbs if possible at the field margins.

A typical seed mix

Name	kg/ha	lb/acre
Perennial rye grass	18	16
Red fescue	5	4½
Crested dog's tail	1	1
Cocksfoot	2	2
Timothy	2	2
Meadow fescue	2	2
Clover	1	1
Total	31	28½

Herbs

Horses enjoy the following herbs in pasture and they are safely consumed in small quantities:

- ✔ Chicory (*Chicorium intybus*)
- ✔ Yarrow (*Achillea millefolium*)
- ✔ Great burnet (*Sanguisorba officinalis*)
- ✔ Dandelion (*Taraxacum officinale*)
- ✔ Ribwort plantain (*Plantago lanceolata*)

PERFECT PASTURES

Pasture plants

Most grasses are more palatable when young, becoming less attractive later in the season or when not sufficiently grazed.

Name	Main qualities
Perennial rye grass (*Lolium perenne*)	Very palatable with good early and late growth
Italian rye grass (*Lolium multiflorum*)	Similar to perennial rye grass but less long lasting
Red fescue, Sheep's fescue (*Festuca rubra, F. ovina*)	Good turf, not highly nutritious
Meadow fescue (*Festuca pratensis*)	Good turf, very palatable, not highly nutritious
Crested dog's tail (*Cyanosurus cristatus*)	Hard wearing
Cocksfoot (*Dactylis glomerata*)	Hard wearing, early and late growth, very palatable
Yorkshire fog (*Holcus lanatus*)	Mid-season grower, not very palatable
Bents (*Agrostis* species)	Good turf, mid-season grower, not highly nutritious
Purple moorgrass, flying bent (*Molina caerulea*)	Grows rapidly, new growth is nutritious
Timothy (*Phleum pratense*)	Very palatable, valuable mid-season grass
Clover (*Trifolium repens, T. pratense*)	Improves soil fertility, drought resistant

From left to right:
White clover
Yorkshire fog
Bent

From left to right:
Sheep's fescue
Red fescue
Meadow fescue

From left to right:
Perennial rye grass
Timothy
Italian rye grass

Ideal stable

Yard design

Consider these features when choosing a livery yard (or designing your own yard). For grazing see p.38–41.

- Approval – is it approved by a recognized body such as the BHS? This means it will meet certain standards.
- Electricity – is there a safe supply and good lighting for dark mornings and evenings?
- Feed room – is it clean, dry and well-organized with a sink and kettle?
- Hay storage – is it separate from stables, dry and well-ventilated?
- Muck heap – is it away from the yard but easily accessed, and regularly cleared/restacked?
- Parking – is there a reasonable place in which to park while attending your horse?
- Safety – is the yard well kept and tidy without hazards that your horse could injure itself on?
- Security – are there good security systems in place? Consider both theft and fire.
- Stables – are they sheltered from prevailing weather? Wind and rain shouldn't blow into the stables.
- Storage – is there a covered area for tools and storage of rugs and bedding, and is it neat and tidy?
- Tack – is there a secure tack room or will you have to take your tack home?
- Turnout – is there plenty of good quality turnout? (See also pp.38–41.)
- Water – is the tap conveniently sited? Are there facilities for soaking hay?
- Yard – is it enclosed with a suitable dry, flat, easy to sweep surface?

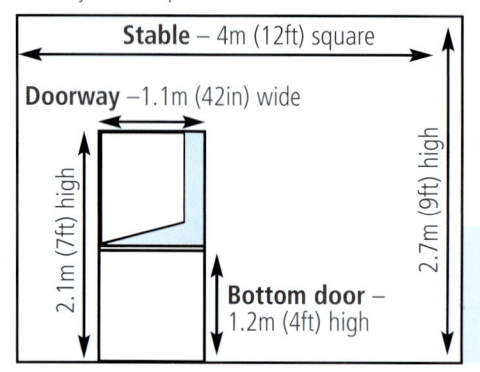

Stable design

There should be:

- Adequate ventilation – roof vent or window (perspex or safety glass). The window should be on the same side as the door to prevent drafts but should not be blocked by the open top door.
- An overhang on the roof or a good gutter – to prevent rain dripping in.
- Solid flooring, preferably roughened concrete, inside and out.
- Floor slope for drainage.
- Safety bolts on the door, including a kick bolt at the bottom.
- Coach hooks to hold the doors open – doors should open outwards.
- Two tie rings – for the horse and the haynet.
- A well-protected light.
- Waterproof light switches well out of the horse's reach.
- Provision for water and feed buckets.

Bedding – a few pros and cons

Shavings – warm, dust-free, highly absorbent, easy to store, relatively cheap, may contain sharp pieces of wood or other rubbish, takes time to rot down.

Hemp – similar to shavings with the same qualities, but more expensive.

Straw – cheap, rots down well, may be eaten, less absorbent than other bedding, more wasteful as difficult to separate clean and dirty, not suitable for horses with respiratory problems.

Paper – warm, dust-free, rots down quickly, some horses are allergic to the ink, very absorbent but becomes heavy when damp, blows around in the yard, expensive.

Rubber matting – warm, dust-free, easy to clean, urine may collect underneath, heavy to lift when necessary.

Stable measurements

These are the ideal for a horse; ponies can manage in slightly smaller stables and may need a lower bottom door.

```
Stable – 4m (12ft) square
Doorway – 1.1m (42in) wide
2.1m (7ft) high
2.7m (9ft) high
Bottom door – 1.2m (4ft) high
```

Perfect manège

The site
If you are lucky enough to have a choice of where to put your manège, consider the following points:
- Access – a surfaced track between stableyard and manège is essential in most cases, not only to prevent poaching from horse traffic but also to allow for maintenance.
- Distractions – seclusion from a busy road and other distractions will ensure better work from the horses.
- Drainage – build at ground level or above for best drainage.
- Electricity – for floodlighting and other uses.
- Fencing – the manège will need to be fenced and gated.
- Gradient – slopes will add to the cost of construction.
- Wind and weather – some shelter will be very much appreciated by all users.

Sizes
A standard manège is 20 x 40m (66 x 130ft), while one designed for international dressage competitions will be 20 x 60m (66 x 200ft). A width of 15m (50ft) is the minimum.

Simple schooling movements
A & B 6 to 20 metre circles and serpentines to improve horse's suppleness
C simple changes of rein across the long diagonals, centre line and halfway line will improve accuracy
D half circles back to the track to change the rein, improve horse suppleness and rider dexterity

Construction
- Site levelled (levelled area at least 1m/3ft bigger than the manège on all sides) and drains and drainage pipes laid.
- Drainage membrane laid over the site.
- Foundation put down – the gravel drainage bed. The stones are around 50mm (2in) and the layer is 120mm (5in) or more.
- Next comes either a layer of smaller gravel for sand surfaces, to prevent the sand filtering into the drainage bed, or another membrane for other surfaces.
- Retaining boards are put in place around the perimeter – they should protrude 150mm (6in) above the school surface.
- The surface is laid.

Surfaces
Sand – cheap, safe and easily maintained. If it is allowed to become dirty (horse manure, fallen leaves), drainage can be a problem. Waxed sand doesn't require watering during dry weather.

Woodchip – a strong, safe and cheap material that provides a good riding surface. It will need topping up annually as it decomposes and full replacement is required after about 6 years.

Granulated pvc – mixed with sand is high maintenance but long-lasting. It produces deeper going than sand and is ideal for young horses.

Rubber (shreds or crumbs) – mixed with sand is excellent for jumping, long-lasting and low maintenance.

Gels – gel surfaces are very expensive but do provide a good surface, especially for jumping.

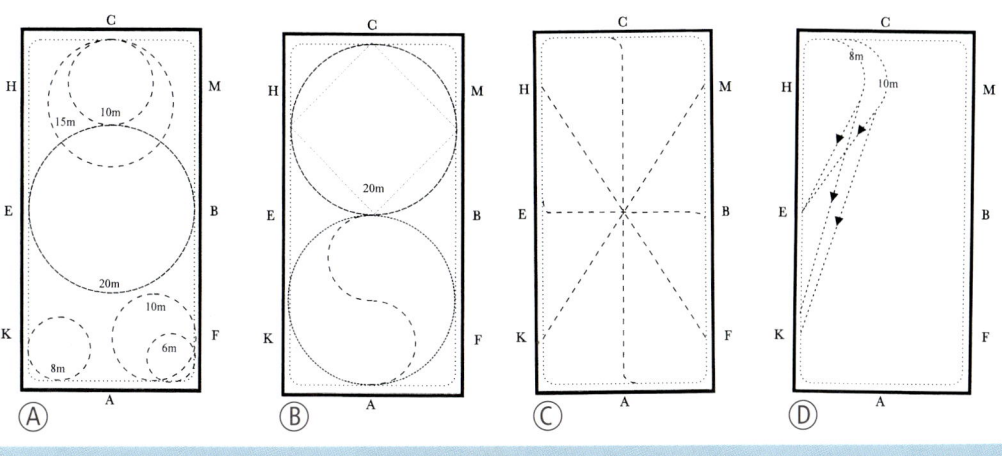

Feet and shoeing

No foot, no horse
Healthy well-cared for feet are vital to your horse's health and comfort as well as his ability to be able to do the work you ask of him.

Feet facts
- Front feet are round to increase their weight-carrying ability. They carry 60% of the horse's weight.
- Back feet are oval to aid propulsion – their main work.
- While the outer horn is non-living, the internal tissues of the feet are extremely sensitive.
- Hooves grow about 5mm (¼in) a month, more in summer less in winter. It takes about 6 months for a the horn to be replaced completely.
- The frog and sole also grow continuously.
- Diet has an influence on the quality of the horn and how fast it grows: grass rings (ridges on the hoof) indicate changes in the levels of nutrition.
- Calcium, zinc, methionine, biotin and sulphur all contribute to healthy horn growth but don't work if given in isolation.
- Most good quality food mixes contain enough nutrients, in the correct balance, to produce healthy horn.
- Shoeing protects the foot, but at the expense of some grip; an unshod horse is less likely to slip, especially on hard ground.

Foot care
- Pick out feet of stabled and grass-kept horses twice a day.
- Check for risen clenches or loose shoes every day.
- Check feet when you return from a ride to ensure nothing has caught in them.
- Keep horses out of very muddy pasture to avoid thrush, mud fever and other problems.
- Consider using hoof disinfectant to prevent foot problems.
- Maintain good stable hygiene to prevent thrush and other foot problems.
- For shod horses arrange for shoeing every 4–6 weeks, possibly more frequently in summer.
- For unshod horses arrange for trimming every 6–10 weeks, more frequently in summer.

Signs of a well-shod horse
- ✔ No light is visible between shoe and hoof.
- ✔ The horn is well trimmed but not dumped.
- ✔ The nails are placed towards the front of the hoof, to enable the heel to expand.
- ✔ The clenches are in a straight line along the hoof about one third of the way up.
- ✔ The clenches and clips are suitably seated.
- ✔ The heels are not too short, nor so long that they pressurize the frog.
- ✔ The horse is sound and moves freely.
- ✔ The shoe sits level on the ground without altering the way the horse stands.

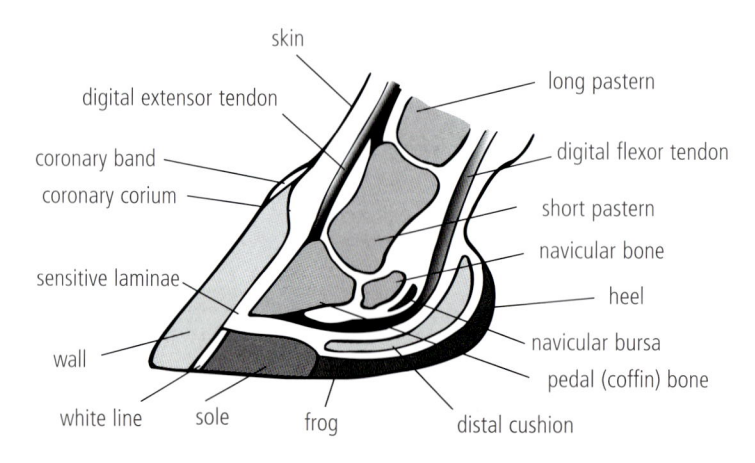

Diagram labels: skin, digital extensor tendon, coronary band, coronary corium, sensitive laminae, wall, white line, sole, frog, distal cushion, pedal (coffin) bone, navicular bursa, heel, navicular bone, short pastern, digital flexor tendon, long pastern

FEET AND SHOEING

Foot problems

Horses can suffer from a variety of foot problems, many of which may be diagnosed and/or treated by the farrier, including:

Abscess – see p.24.

Bruised sole – see p.28.

Corns – see p.28.

Sand cracks Vertical cracks in the hoof, sometimes caused by allowing feet to grow overlong. Shallow cracks can be treated by trimming and balancing the hoof; clips may be used to prevent them growing longer. Deep sand cracks can cause lameness and may have to be opened up and cut back to healthy horn along their length; the two sides of the crack may then be wired together or a bar shoe used.

Seedy toe Bacteria or fungi infect the white line, causing softening and crumbling, usually in the toe. Laminitis, infrequent trimming or stone damage may all be factors. The infected horn is cut back to healthy tissue, and remedial shoeing is often used.

Thrush – see p.24.

Some definitions

- **Bar shoe** – a shoe with closed heels for remedial shoeing, in cases of laminitis or fractured pedal bones, for example.
- **Cast** – a shoe that has come off.
- **Clench** – the bent over end of the nail in the hoof. Raised clenches stand proud of the hoof.
- **Clip** – a raised piece of metal drawn from the shoe to help keep it in position. There are usually two clips on a back shoe and one on a front shoe.
- **Dumped** – an over-rasped hoof.
- **Fullering** – the groove in the underside of the shoe, put there to improve grip and make the shoe lighter.
- **Nail** – used to fasten the shoe, the nail should sit comfortably in the nail hole. Traditionally, 3 nails are used on the inside and 4 on the outside, but the farrier will decide how many are necessary.
- **Nail bind or prick** – is when the newly inserted nail touches the sensitive part of the foot, causing lameness.
- **Plain stamped shoe** – a shoe without fullering, usually used for draught horses.
- **Remove** – a shoe that is reused, being replaced once the foot is trimmed.
- **Rolled toe shoe** – a shoe without clips and with the toe curved upwards to encourage a quick break over (the hoof leaving the ground) and reduce the risk of over-reaching.
- **Seat** – a small indentation made in the horn so that the clips and clenches fit flush with the rest of the hoof.

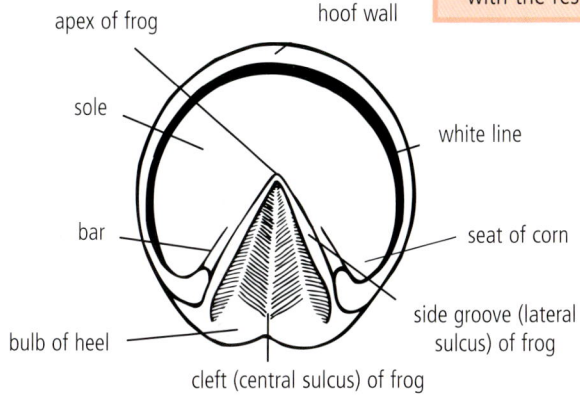

Saddles

Fit tips

Explain clearly what you want from your saddle when making the appointment with the saddler.

If your saddle is reflocked or adjusted in any way, your saddler must check it on your horse.

You and your horse can and should feel comfortable – if you don't like the saddle then it's no good.

Taking and using a wither pattern

✦ Use a flexicurve or flexible wire, such as a wire coat hanger.
✦ Place the flexicurve over the top of the withers.
✦ Shape it over the withers and around the shoulders. Smooth it all along its length, making sure you follow the contours exactly. Do one side then get someone to hold the curve in place while you move to the other (below left).
✦ Draw the resulting curve on a sheet of paper, noting nearside and offside – this is the wither pattern (below centre).
✦ Draw the curve onto cardboard and cut out the shape – this is the template.
✦ Get someone to hold up the saddle with the pommel towards you and fit the template into the saddle, lining it up with the points of the tree (below right).
✦ The saddle panels should fit snugly but not tightly around the template.
✦ There should be three fingers clearance into the pommel.

Fit checklist

- The front of the saddle sits 1cm (½in) behind the shoulder blade.
- The back of the saddle ends 15cm (6in) from the loin whorls.
- It touches the horse's back all along its length when girthed up.
- From the back of the saddle, slip your hand, palm downwards, under the panel. Beginning near the stirrup bar, run your hand backwards. There should be no restriction and the pressure should be even all along.
- The seat is horizontal to the ground.
- The cantle is slightly higher than the pommel.
- You can see through the length of the channel from front to back and its edges do not touch the backbone.
- The horse's shoulder is completely free to move naturally as he walks.

Signs of a poor fit

✘ Saddle slopes to front or slips forward in use – too wide.
✘ Saddle slopes to back – too narrow.
✘ Pinches, scuffed hair or uneven sweatmarks visible when the saddle is removed.
✘ The horse's performance is affected – reluctant go downhill, uneven shoe wear, takes a dislike to saddle.

A good saddle has:

✔ a wide weight-bearing surface – wide panels;
✔ smooth, soft, flat panels – run your fingers along their surface;
✔ a channel that is about 6cm (2½in) wide along its whole length;
✔ symmetry – above and below.

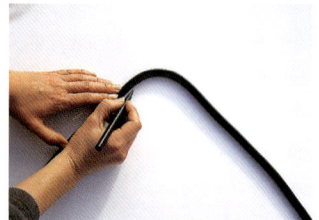

SADDLES

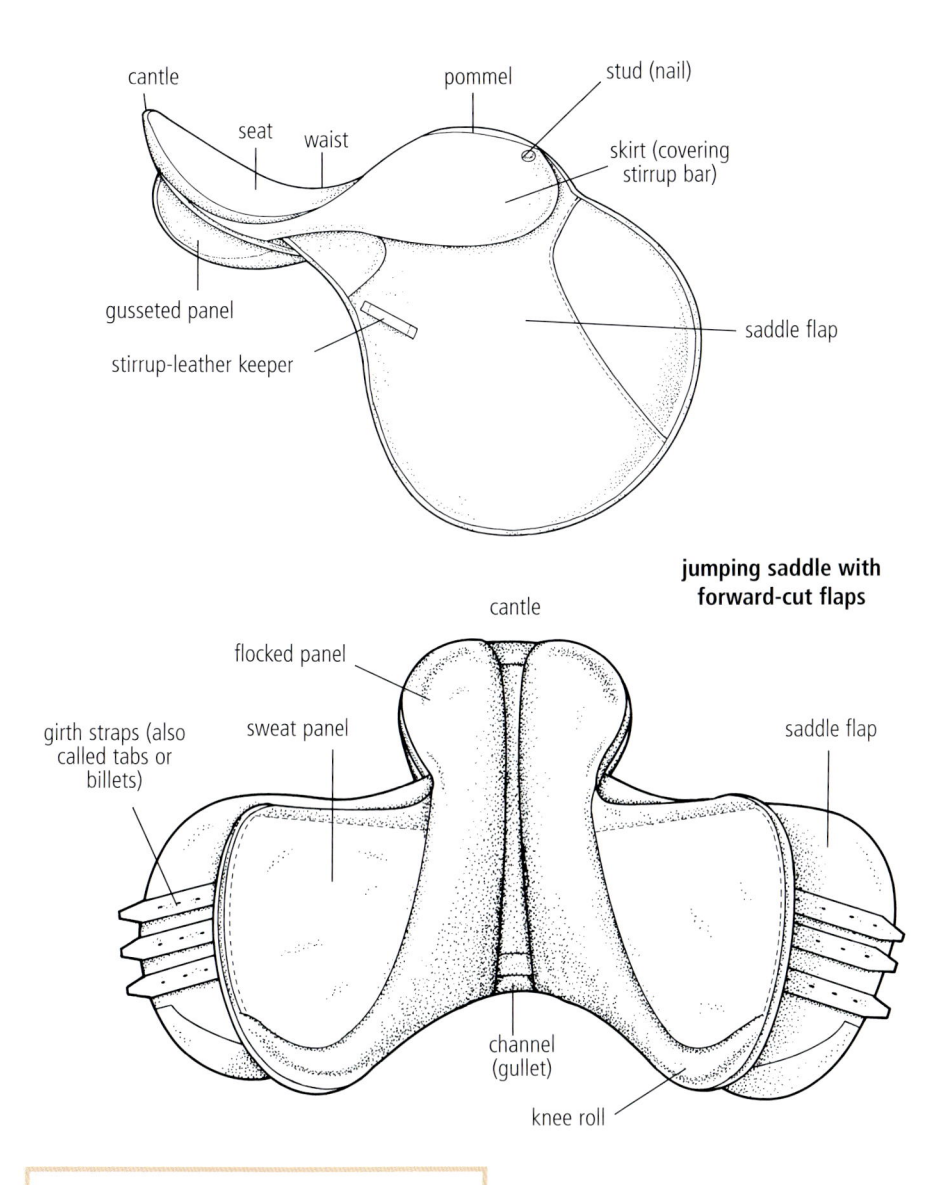

Labels on upper illustration:
- cantle
- seat
- waist
- pommel
- stud (nail)
- skirt (covering stirrup bar)
- gusseted panel
- stirrup-leather keeper
- saddle flap

jumping saddle with forward-cut flaps

Labels on lower illustration:
- flocked panel
- cantle
- sweat panel
- saddle flap
- girth straps (also called tabs or billets)
- channel (gullet)
- knee roll

Saddle measurements
Width is the distance between the points of the tree.
Length is the measurement from the centre of the tree stud (nail) to the centre of the cantle.

Stirrup size
Ensure there is a 1cm (½in) gap between the riding boot and stirrup on each side.

Western saddles
Most of the fit checklist points (left) are relevant to fitting a Western saddle. Like an English saddle, a Western saddle should fit at the withers with clearance over the length of the backbone. It should not rub on the loins.

Bridles

Fitting a bridle
- Approximate sizes: pony to 14hh; cob 14–15hh; full 15–17hh.
- The browband fits around the brow without pulling at the back of the ears (too short) or slipping or flapping at the front (too long).
- The throatlash is done up loosely so that you can fit your hand's width between the horse's cheek and the throatlash (below left).
- A cavesson noseband sits one to two finger's width below the cheekbone and two fingers can slip between it and the horse's face (below right).
- A drop noseband sits 7cm (3in) above the horse's nostrils and one finger can slip between it and the horse's muzzle. It is vital not to have it too low as it will restrict the horse's breathing.
- Flash nosebands fit in the same way as a cavesson, with the flash strap buckled at the back of the jaw and tight enough to allow one finger to slip between it and the horse's muzzle.
- The bit should be high enough in the mouth to give the horse a slight smile, not a grimace. Check its width by straightening it gently in the horse's mouth – you should be able to fit your little finger between the bit cheekpiece and the horse's lips on both sides.

Bit size
Straighten the bit and measure from the inside of one cheekpiece to the inside of the other.

Fitting a curb chain
The chain sits gently in the chin groove at the back of the jaw and comes into action when the curb cheeks are drawn back by 45 degrees.
- Attach the end link to the offside curb hook.
- Holding the chain at both ends, twist it clockwise until the links lie flat and the flylink hangs down.
- Hook the last link to the nearside curb hook.
- Check fit by pulling back gently on the reins.
- Unhook and use the next link in if necessary, keeping the links flat.

Martingales
- Martingale neck straps should fit near the withers and be loose enough to allow a hand's width between strap and wither.
- Standing martingale – with the horse's head in the correct position, lift the martingale up towards the neck. It should just reach the throat.
- Running martingale – with the martingale attached at the girth, bring both rings to one side of the horse's neck; they should reach the withers.

Tack cleaning tips
- ✔ Use a damp cloth to wipe off mud.
- ✔ Use washing up liquid and water sparingly on very greasy areas; rinse well and allow to dry.
- ✔ Use saddle soap to feed, as well as clean.
- ✔ Use a clean dry cloth to produce a shine.
- ✔ Periodically, use leather dressing, but not on flocked panels as it spoils 'loft'.

BRIDLES

snaffle bridle

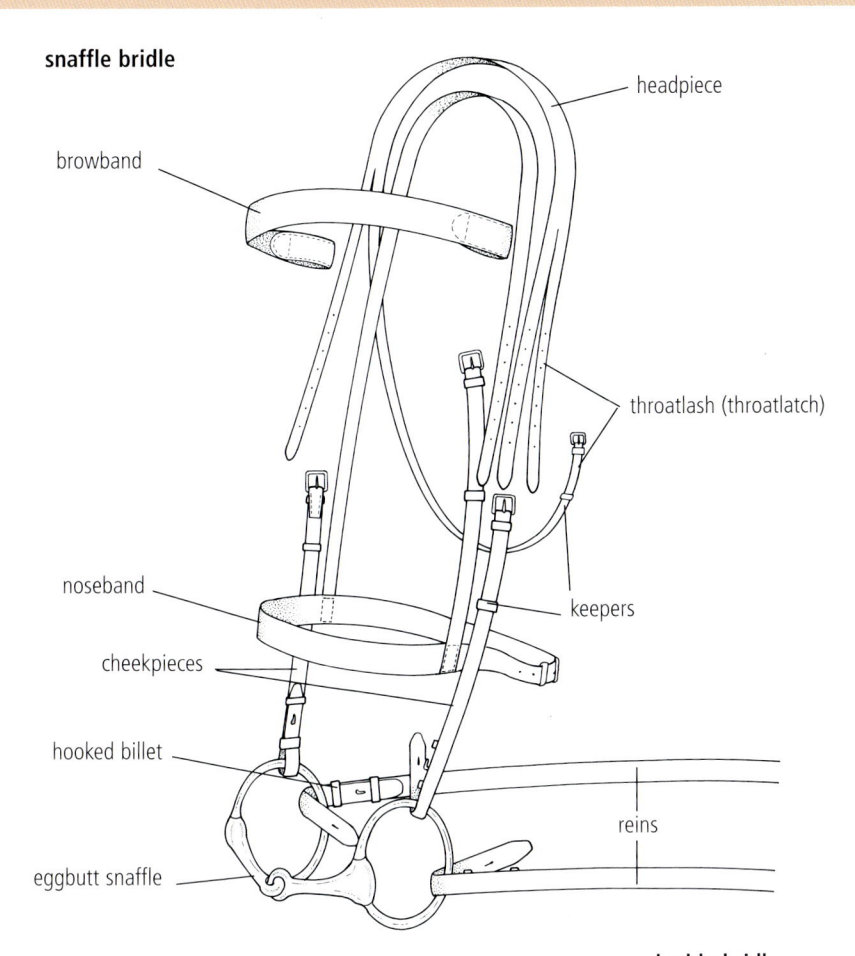

- headpiece
- browband
- throatlash (throatlatch)
- noseband
- keepers
- cheekpieces
- hooked billet
- reins
- eggbutt snaffle

double bridle

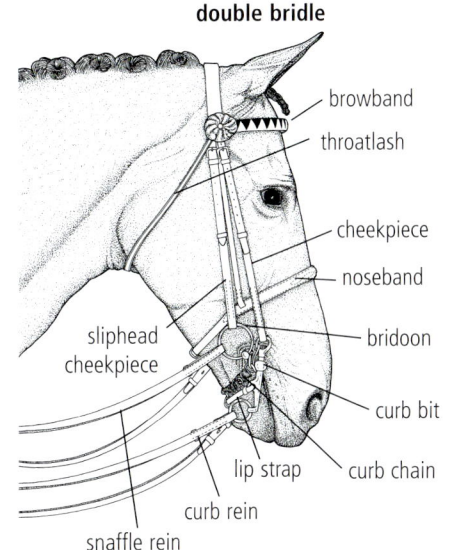

- browband
- throatlash
- cheekpiece
- noseband
- bridoon
- sliphead cheekpiece
- curb bit
- lip strap
- curb chain
- curb rein
- snaffle rein

Double bridle

A double bridle has:
- two bits: a bridoon (a light snaffle) and a curb;
- a second headpiece (a sliphead) with one cheekpiece (on off side). This fits under the headpiece and secures the bridoon, while the curb bit is secured on the bridle cheekpieces;
- a lip strap to hold the curb chain should it become detached and to prevent the horse grabbing the cheeks of the curb bit;
- two sets of reins, one for each bit.

Fit a double bridle in the same way as a snaffle bridle (see left) but:
- make the throatlash marginally looser;
- lower the noseband very slightly;
- fit the bridoon above the curb – slightly higher in the mouth than a single bit would be.

A guide to riding terms

Canter (**lope**) is a pace with three beats and a moment of suspension: in canter the beats are even – 1,2,3 1,2,3 – in lope they are uneven – 1, 2-3, 1, 2-3. Right lead is left hind, left fore and right hind together, right fore, suspension. Left lead is right hind, right fore and left hind together, left fore, suspension. Canter on a right lead when riding clockwise, a left lead when riding anti-clockwise. Counter canter is when these leads are reversed in advanced work; false canter is when this happens unintentionally. The lead can be seen by the rider as a more pronounced forward and backward movement of the leading shoulder: in left lead this is seen in the left shoulder.

Collection is seen in trot and canter, and variations on these paces, such as piaffe and passage. The horse's strides are shortened until they become very light and springy. The horse feels very agile and manoeuvrable.

Contact is the link between the horse's mouth and the rider's hands through the reins. A horse must accept contact before he can learn to be on the bit, while the rider must learn to ride in balance, without leaning on the reins, and develop 'soft' giving hands.

Diagonals Trot on the right diagonal when going anti-clockwise (to the left) and on the left diagonal when going clockwise (to the right). Trotting on the right diagonal involves sitting when the horse's right fore and left hind touch the ground and rising as they leave the ground – this can be seen by the rider as the horse's right shoulder moving backward (foot touching the ground) then forward (leaving the ground). Rise as the outside shoulder moves forward and sit as it moves back.

Extended paces are where the horse covers the most ground at walk, trot and canter by taking longer strides at greater speed than the medium or working paces while maintaining the same rhythm.

Flying change is where the canter lead is changed from right to left, or vice versa, without altering the pace or rhythm. The change is requested by altering the leg aids during the moment of suspension.

Gallop, the fastest pace, has four rapid beats. Right lead gallop is left hind, right hind, left fore, right fore, suspension. Left lead is right hind, left hind, right fore, left fore, suspension.

Half pass is where the horse, bent around the rider's inside leg and in the direction of travel, moves sideways and forwards on the diagonal making two tracks. The forehand is slightly ahead of the quarters. The outside legs cross in front of the inside legs so if the direction of movement is left to right the left legs cross in front of the right legs. Half pass is performed in collected trot or collected canter.

Impulsion is created by the rider's legs, so that the horse feels as if it has boundless, contained energy coming from the quarters.

In front of the leg is when the horse accepts and reponds instantly to the lightest leg aids, without rushing and remaining in balance.

Inside leg and/or hand is nearest the centre of the school. On a circle or turn the horse bends around the inside leg.

Jog is a Western trot in slow-time with less knee action than in a dressage-type trot.

Leg yield The horse moves both sideways and forwards with the inside legs crossing in front of the outside legs; there is a slight bend at the poll. Performed in either walk or working trot.

Medium paces are between working and extended. While the speed and rhythm remain the same as in the working pace, the stride lengthens so increasing the ground covered. In medium walk the horse should overtrack.

On the bit A horse is on the bit when his energy is coming through from his hindquarters to the forehand, which is light. He accepts the bit softly, his neck arched and raised but supple, and he is in self-carriage, making a rounded, powerful and elegant outline.

Outside leg and/or hand is the one nearest the outer edge of the school. On a circle or turn the outside leg acts behind the girth to encourage the quarters in the turn.

A GUIDE TO RIDING TERMS

Passage is a rhythmic, collected and springy trot; each diagonal pair of feet is lifted very high and the moment of suspension is prolonged.

Piaffe is a springy trot performed on the spot, rhythmically and with great collection.

Rein back is almost two-time (like trot) with diagonal pairs of legs moving back together.

Renvers/travers (haunches out, haunches in) The horse moves forwards and sideways with the quarters out (renvers) or in (travers), bending around the rider's leg and making four tracks. The difference between the two is only in the horse's original position: in renvers his forehand leaves the track, in travers his quarters leave the track.

Self-carriage is where a horse carries himself lightly and in balance with more of his weight on his haunches so that he is able to take the additional weight of a rider and perform school movements without falling onto his forehand.

Shoulder in is where the horse bends around the rider's inside leg, bringing the forehand off the straight line so making three tracks with the inside fore crossing in front of the outside fore. The trot must be at least slightly collected.

Tracking up is when the horse's hind feet step into the tracks made by his forefeet in walk. Overtracking, where the hind feet over step the tracks by anything up to 30cm (12in), is an indicator of a good, long-striding, free walk. An under tracking horse is likely to be young or unschooled, while hind foot prints to one side of the forefoot prints may indicate stiffness.

Trot is a pace with two even beats. Diagonal pairs of feet touch the ground together: the sequence is right fore and left hind, suspension, left fore and right hind, suspension.

Turn on the forehand is when the horse's hindquarters turn around the forehand at walk. If the quarters move right, the left hindleg crosses in front of the right hindleg; if they move left, the right hindleg crosses in front of the left hindleg. The forelegs step on the spot while the hindlegs describe part of a circle.

Turn on the haunches or pirouette is when the horse's forehand turns around the quarters at walk or canter. The inside hind foot is the pivot around which the forelegs and outside hind foot move. The outside foreleg crosses in front of the inside foreleg, while the outside hind moves around the inside hind which returns to more or less the same spot each time it is lifted.

Walk is a pace with four even beats, like a march: a sequence is left hind, left fore, right hind, right fore. There are always at least two feet on the ground.

Working paces are trot and canter performed at a steady rhythm, balance and speed. They are used for schooling horses as yet untrained in medium, extended and collected paces.

A brief guide to jumps

An **arrowhead** looks like a triangle when viewed from above. The horse has to jump into it via the point, and then jump out.

A **bounce** is two or more jumps in a row positioned closely with no non-jumping strides in between, so the horse lands and immediately takes off again.

A **coffin** is a combination of jumps involving a rail to jump in, a ditch on lower ground and a rail to jump out.

A **corner** forms a V-shape. Both arms of the V are cleared together near its point.

A **drop** is any jump that involves landing on ground lower than that you took off from.

A **Normandy bank** is a combination of a jump up onto a flat bank and a jump out over a rail with a drop on the far side.

An **oxer** is a wide jump with rails, a hedge and possibly a ditch.

A **parallel** is two sets of rails at the same height (unlike a staircase).

A **pyramid** is any jump where the middle section is highest, as in a tiger trap.

A **spread** is a wide jump.

A **staircase** is a jump consisting of two or more bars with the back bar(s) higher than the front one(s).

A **tiger trap** is formed with two sets of rails sloping so that they lean against each other, making an upside down V-shape when viewed from the side.

A **trakehner** is an upright with a ditch under it.

An **upright** is a simple single jump.

Schooling

Most people want to enjoy riding their horse, whether that pleasure comes from a leisurely ride in the countryside or jumping competitively at a high level or just popping over an occasional fence. Underpinning each rider's enjoyment is their ability to control and direct their horse. The horse needs to be balanced, obedient, responsive, supple and co-ordinated. The rider has to be able to manoeuvre the horse's forehand, move the quarters over, take one step here and so on. All this is possible if the horse is well schooled.

The amount of schooling your horse receives during a week usually depends on the discipline you are interested in and the amount of time you have. Your horse's wellbeing is dependent on you providing variety and stimulation for him through his work, as well as creating a good balance between work and play, so even if you are planning to specialise in dressage, it's important not to overdo the training – he needs time at liberty and he will appreciate hacks out and jumping sessions, along with his flatwork.

Schooling sessions should not be overlong, especially if you are working with a young horse: 20–30 minutes is usually fine for a youngster. With any horse, make sure you finish the session on a good note.

SEEKING A CONTACT

It's a good sign if your horse is wet in his mouth as it indicates that he has been seeking a contact with the bit.

WORKING OUT A TYPICAL SESSION

A schooling session can be divided into four phases:
- Warm up
- Work
- New work – introducing new manoeuvres (this phase may be omitted if either you or your horse are not working particularly well)
- Cool down

Tips for successful schooling

- To give structure to your long-term schooling, look at the levels of dressage tests to see when various movements are introduced. This will suggest a logical progression for your training.
- If you need to make a correction to your horse's way of going, do so, but immediately soften your hand and encourage him to go forwards.
- If your horse has a problem with balance, try lungeing him. Done correctly, this will help him to establish his balance before he has to deal with the added problem of a rider. Lungeing also provides you with the opportunity of seeing how he moves.
- Make sure that your horse is completely comfortable before you begin, otherwise you will achieve nothing. For example, stiffness through his back leads to poor transitions, which will affect all other movements.
- Take frequent breaks during a schooling session so your horse can relax and stretch. If you work him in an outline for too long, his muscles may ache (especially if he is unused to the work) and you'll only make him resistant. Allowing him a break to stretch also acts as a reward for him.

SHOULDER-IN

If your horse is inexperienced at lateral work or you are finding shoulder-in difficult, try starting with shoulder-fore. Use your inside rein to create bend and your outside rein to bring the shoulders off the track. Your inside leg asks for the sideways movement and your outside hand also controls the speed. Once your horse can continue in shoulder-fore along the length of the school easily on both reins, you can progress to shoulder-in.

Do this by asking for more bend and increasing the angle until the full 30-degree three-track movement of shoulder-in is achieved.

Taken from The Photographic Guide to Schooling Your Horse by Lesley Bayley. Published by David & Charles, ISBN 0 7153 1386 X.

January

Let me lead my life in the saddle,
It's the life to which I've been bred;
It's the life of the wise
With only the skies,
The wonderful skies, overhead.

Sir Michael William Selby Bruce *My Choice in Life*

22nd Dec FARRIER.

December/January 2005

Monday 27

Tuesday 28

Wednesday 29

Thursday 30

Friday 31
15 x HAY Pd.

Saturday 1 — New Year's Day

Sunday 2
Field Rent
Pd to date

- Decide on your aims and ambitions for the year
- Look out for rug rubs, adjusting fit if necessary

January 2005

Monday 3 — Bank Holiday, UK & Rep of Ireland

Tuesday 4 — Bank Holiday, Scotland

Wednesday 5

Thursday 6

Friday 7

Saturday 8

Sunday 9

● Look out for frozen water troughs

Fld Rnt Pc

January 2005

Monday 10

Tuesday 11

Wednesday 12

Thursday 13

Friday 14

Saturday 15

Sunday 16

● Monitor your horse's weight (p.34), increasing hay and feed if necessary

January 2005

Monday 17

Tuesday 18

Wednesday 19

Thursday 20

Friday 21

Saturday 22

Sunday 23 *PIP HOME*

- Watch for mud fever (p.29), rainscald (p.30), thrush (p.24)

January 2005

Monday 24

Tuesday 25

Wednesday 26

Thursday 27
Australia Day
Desert Circuit begins (ends 14 March)

Friday 28

Saturday 29

Sunday 30

- On freezing mornings give extra hay to grass-kept horses

February

A good horse is never a bad colour.

Anonymous

January/February 2005

Monday 31

Tuesday 1
* £100 Laura + Karina into POT!
£10 to Karina for carrots.

Wednesday 2
HAY x 15 Pd from Pot.

Thursday 3

Friday 4

Saturday 5
HORSES WORMED ours Pd from Pot.
Tammy Pd

Sunday 6

Pd Rent Pd

- Watch for mud fever (p.29), rainscald (p.30), thrush (p.24)
- Watch for rug rubs, adjusting fit if necessary

February 2005   SNOW PART WEEK

Monday 7

Tuesday 8

Wednesday 9

Thursday 10

Friday 11

Saturday 12

Sunday 13

- Look out for frozen water troughs
- Book the equine dentist (p.20)

SNOW ALL WEEK

February 2005

Monday 14
St Valentine's Day

Tuesday 15

Wednesday 16
FARRIER   £15 x 3 from Pot. + £2 for look at Pip.
Extra for Lukes shoes direct from L.

Thursday 17
20 x HAY   Pd from Pot

Friday 18

Saturday 19

Sunday 20
60 Bales of hay (£100) from Derek Bond
(Bad weather on way - needs to get sheep in for lambing)
£100 to pay back to Laura (holiday money)

- Check your horse's vaccinations are up-to-date (p.12)
- Administer late winter wormer, if necessary (p.13)

Fld Rnt Pd

February 2005

SNOW ALL WEEK

Monday 21

Tuesday 22

Wednesday 23

Thursday 24

Friday 25

Saturday 26

Sunday 27

- Monitor your horse's weight (p.34), increasing hay and feed if necessary
- On freezing mornings give extra hay to grass-kept horses

SNOW ALL WEEK **February/March 2005**

Monday 28 Tammy owes £83: for Feb outstanding
£82 Pd 9/3/05

Tuesday 1 £100 Rent owed from tammy for March Rent.
plus any hay - 6 biscuits per day.
£100 L + £100 K FOR POT.   £3 to k for Carrots

Wednesday 2

Thursday 3

Friday 4

Saturday 5

Sunday 6 Mothering Sunday

- Change to a lighter rug on warm dry days

Pd Rent Pd

March

A demon to handle! a devil to ride!
Small wonder the surcingle burst;
You'd have thought that he'd buck himself out of his hide
On the morning we saddled him first.

Harry Morant *Who's Riding Old Harlequin Now?*

March 2005

Monday 7

Tuesday 8

Wednesday 9
TAMMY
c/o
SAM PD £82:

Thursday 10

Friday 11

Saturday 12

Sunday 13

- Change to a lighter rug on warm dry days

Fld Rnt-Pd

March 2005

Monday 14

Tuesday 15

Wednesday 16 — SAM PD £7650

Thursday 17 — St Patrick's Day, Bank Holiday Rep of Ireland

Friday 18

Saturday 19

Sunday 20 — TAMMY TOLD ROSIE MUST MOVE BY END OF APRIL

- Check for emerging ragwort and other poisonous plants (p.31)

March 2005

Monday 21

Tuesday 22

Wednesday 23

Thursday 24

Friday 25
Good Friday, Bank Holiday UK & Rep of Ireland

Saturday 26

Sunday 27
Easter Day
Grand Prix of Tampa, British Summer Time begins

● Start spring worming programme (p.13)

March/April 2005

Monday 28 — Easter Monday, Bank Holiday UK and Rep of Ireland

Tuesday 29

Wednesday 30 — SAM PD £61!

Thursday 31 — 10 HAY (PD FROM POT)

Friday 1 — FARRIER (a.m.)

£100 K+L Pd to post

Saturday 2 — Budweiser American Invitational Grand Prix

Sunday 3 — HORSES WORMED =(x2)

Pd Vet (
Pd

April

He stretches to the gallop
And feels the prairie grasses
Crisply give to his going
And spring up as he passes...

Anonymous *The Adam and Eve of the Mustangs: Texas 1540*

April 2005

Monday 4

Tuesday 5
Pip Vets - Scan.

Wednesday 6

Thursday 7

Friday 8

Saturday 9

Sunday 10

- Harrow and roll pastures (p.38)

Fld Rnt Pd

April 2005

Monday 11

Tuesday 12 Rosie Sold - Moved.

Wednesday 13 10x HAY

Thursday 14

Friday 15

Saturday 16

Sunday 17 JACOB IN.

- Beware of grazing conditions that are likely to induce laminitis (p.25)
- Continue worming as necessary (p.13)

Ad Rnt Pd

April 2005

Monday 18

Tuesday 19

Wednesday 20

Thursday 21

Friday 22

Saturday 23 Charge to Denise — JACOB — Week Ending
Livery - Rent plus 'shifts' £35:00
Hay" £5:00   TOTAL £40:00
Pd in full 26/4/05

Sunday 24

- Change to a lighter rug on warm dry days, leave rugs off in really nice weather
- Check for ragwort and other poisonous plants (p.31)

Pd Rent Pd.

April/May 2005

Monday 25

Tuesday 26

Wednesday 27 MY BIRTHDAY

Thursday 28

Friday 29

Saturday 30
Charge to Denise - Jacob
Livery - Rent £15 + 25
ROSIE DEADLINE. Hay " £5.
6 BALES OF HAY w/e
Pd.
TOTAL £~~45~~ 45!

Sunday 1
£2.50 carried over we owe D.

Jacob 2 bales   £100 k+L Pd to pdr

- Brush your horse regularly to remove loose hair

Pd Rent Pd

May

There is no secret so close as that between a rider and his horse.

R.S. Surtees *Mr Sponge's Sporting Tour*

May 2005

Monday 2 — Early May Bank Holiday UK & Rep of Ireland

Tuesday 3

Wednesday 4
Farrier to Jacob 4.15pm.

Thursday 5 — Badminton Horse Trials begins (to be confirmed)

Friday 6

Saturday 7
charge to Denise £15 + £20   − £2.50
2 bales of hay given 1/5/05   £5:00   £17.50
FARRIER = £25:00
                        TOTAL £62-50p

Sunday 8 — Badminton Horse Trials ends (to be confirmed)
Charged for M PM TUE WED PM
TH AM. FRI SAT PM. (−2.50)
                £65 Pd to K

- Remove rugs, repair and clean them

Pd Rwr Pd

May 2005

Monday 9

Tuesday 10

Wednesday 11

Thursday 12

Friday 13

Saturday 14
Cheurge to D £15 + 32.50 (-2.50) = £45
Worm count £11.84   Feed £9-
Wormer £12.50   Hay £2.50
                                          TOTAL £80.84

Sunday 15

● Monitor your horse's weight (p.34), reduce grazing and feed if necessary

Fld Rur Pol

May 2005

Monday 16 — Farrier 4pm   EQUEST All horses wormed

Tuesday 17

Wednesday 18

Thursday 19

Friday 20

Saturday 21

Sunday 22

- Check for ragwort and other poisonous plants (p.31)

Fld Rub Pd

Karina in process of buying Big J.

May 2005

Monday 23

Tuesday 24

Wednesday 25

Thursday 26

Friday 27

Saturday 28

Sunday 29

May/June 2005

Spring Bank Holiday UK, Memorial Day USA

Monday 30

Tuesday 31

Wednesday 1
HORSE TRAILER INS. £105!
Pd from pot.
£100 L £125 K Pd to Pot

Thursday 2

Friday 3

Saturday 4

Sunday 5
Sponsored Ride

- Remove rugs, repair and clean them

Pd Pot Pd

June

For you were our care from the day you were foaled,
A quaint little creature, so leggy and shy,
To grow like your dam, most courageous and bold...

Edric Roberts *Four-Year-Old*

June 2005

Monday 6

Tuesday 7

Wednesday 8

Thursday 9

Friday 10

Saturday 11

Sunday 12

- Check water troughs for cleanliness, removing algae and dead vegetation

June 2005

Monday 13

Tuesday 14

Wednesday 15

Thursday 16

Friday 17

Saturday 18

Sunday 19 — Father's Day, Paint Horse World Show begins

- Monitor your horse's weight (p.34), reduce grazing and feed if necessary

June 2005

Monday 20

Tuesday 21

Wednesday 22

Thursday 23

Friday 24

Saturday 25

Sunday 26

- Give your horse a bath on a warm dry still day

June/July 2005

Monday 27 — Farrier 4pm

Tuesday 28

Wednesday 29 — 100 Bales of Hay from Derek @ £1.75 (£175.)

Thursday 30

Friday 1

Saturday 2 — £100 L + £125 k Pd to Pat   £175 Repaid to L for hay   £152 for a pot
Paint Horse World Show ends

Sunday 3

● Check water troughs for cleanliness, removing algae and dead vegetation

Pd Pat Pd
Pd Pat Pd

July

One white foot, buy a horse,
Two white feet, try a horse,
Three white feet, look well about him,
Four white feet, go without him!

Anonymous

July 2005

Monday 4

Tuesday 5

Wednesday 6

Thursday 7

Friday 8

Saturday 9

Sunday 10

- Get ready for hay/haylage making

Hd Rent Pd

July 2005

Monday 11

Tuesday 12

Wednesday 13

Thursday 14

Friday 15

Saturday 16

Sunday 17

● Book the equine dentist

Ha Rent Pd

July 2005

Monday 18

Tuesday 19

Wednesday 20

Thursday 21

Friday 22

Saturday 23 — Tevis Cup (Western States Trail Ride) begins

Karina hols (2wks)

Sunday 24

Ha Rent Pd

● Give your horse a bath on a warm dry still day

July 2005

Monday 25 — Due Worming (10 wks)

Tuesday 26

Wednesday 27

Thursday 28

Friday 29

Saturday 30

Sunday 31

Hd Rent Pd

August

When God created Horses...
He took some tireless muscle
And mingled it with brain.

He added grace and carriage
And a sure foot, agile gait
With a sense of noble bearing
And courage as a trait.

G.A. Brant *A Gift to Man*

August 2005

Bank Holiday Scotland, Public Holiday Rep of Ireland, Civic Holiday USA

Monday 1
£125 Pd to Por K.
£100 Pd to Por L.
Horses wormed
Equest
Pd from pot.

Tuesday 2

Wednesday 3

Thursday 4

Friday 5

Saturday 6
FARRIER 2.30 - Pd from pot 4x trims.
(£18 owed to L for Pip's fronts by K)

Sunday 7
Karina home.

- Check water troughs for cleanliness, removing algae and dead vegetation

August 2005

Monday 8

Tuesday 9

Wednesday 10

Thursday 11 — Laura hols 2 wks.

Friday 12

Saturday 13

Sunday 14

● Buy new rugs

August 2005

Monday 15

Tuesday 16

Wednesday 17

Thursday 18

Friday 19

Saturday 20

Sunday 21

- Clean and repair rugs

August 2005

Monday 22

Tuesday 23   J.C. Rugged night.

Wednesday 24

Thursday 25 Laura home

Friday 26

Saturday 27

Sunday 28

- Watch out for bot fly eggs

August/September 2005

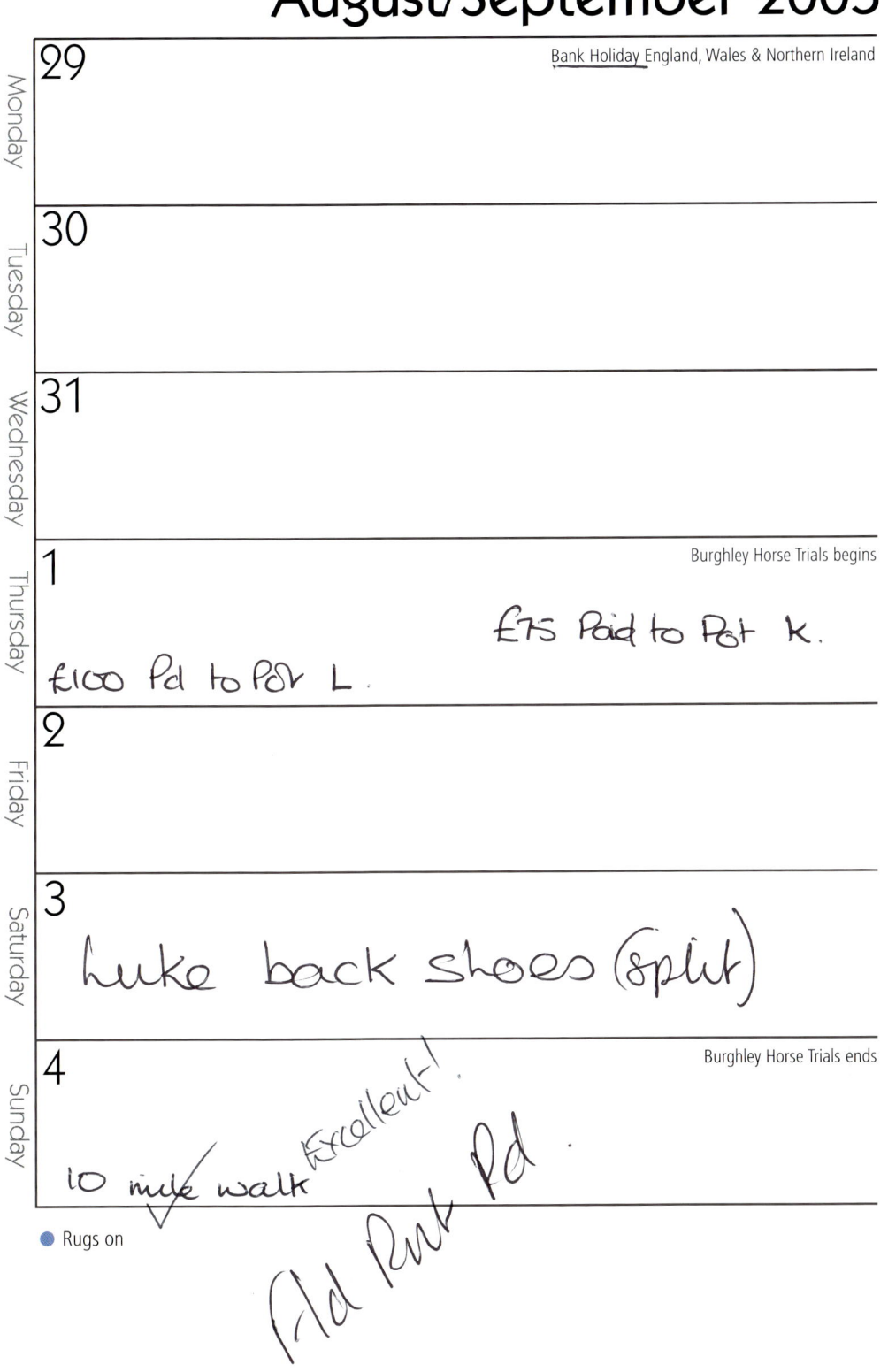

Monday 29 — Bank Holiday England, Wales & Northern Ireland

Tuesday 30

Wednesday 31

Thursday 1 — Burghley Horse Trials begins
£100 Pd to Pet L.   £75 Paid to Pet K.

Friday 2

Saturday 3
Luke back shoes (split)

Sunday 4 — Burghley Horse Trials ends
10 mile walk Excellent!
Old Rnk Pd.

● Rugs on

September

Let oil, not steam, nor wings of dream deprive us of our own –
The wide world for a kingdom and the saddle for a throne!

Will H. Ogilvie *The Horseman*

September 2005

Monday 5 £10 Pd by Angie/Nicole for Jake.

Tuesday 6

Wednesday 7

Thursday 8

Friday 9

Saturday 10

Sunday 11 — Grandparents' Day USA

Pd Pd Pd

- Plan your clipping calendar

September 2005

Monday 12 £10 Pd Nicole

Luke rugged night

Tuesday 13

Wednesday 14 ✶ TET/FLU + TEETH.
(Jake sedated) All pd. (see bottom)

Thursday 15

Friday 16

Saturday 17

Sunday 18

Pld Rent Pd

🌕 Beware of grazing conditions that are likely to induce laminitis (p.25)

September 2005

Monday 19 £10 Pd Nicole

Tuesday 20 Day off work — Luke to Slindon on own!! Something learnt Point trailer toward home!

Wednesday 21 farrier 3pm.

Thursday 22

Friday 23

Saturday 24

Sunday 25 Pd Rent Pd

• Watch out for bot fly eggs

TET & FLU INJ DUE & DENTISTRY
(Karina owes £29 to Laura) Pd

September/October 2005

Monday 26 — £10 Pd Nicole

Tuesday 27

Wednesday 28

Thursday 29

Friday 30

Ftd Rent - Paid

Saturday 1 — Start pay monthly rent. Started feeding Luke - (build-up) £130 months pay. K = £175 Pd to pet L = £100 Pd to pet

Sunday 2 — Paid (£100 chq(L) + £30) Covers 1st Oct to 31st Oct

● Administer wormer, particularly for tapeworm (or October) (p.13)

October

Gifted with spirit – the pluck of his dam;
Made of the tendon and bone of his sire;
Playful as a kitten and kind as a lamb,
Good-looking withal – what more d'ye require?

G.A. Fothergill *'Bonnington'* – a Four-Year-Old Chestnut

October 2005

Monday 3 — Nic Pd

Tuesday 4

Wednesday 5

Thursday 6

Friday 7

Saturday 8

Sunday 9 — Rest Pd   Slindon Luke + Jake (ROVER!).

- Rugs on
- Wear high visibility kit when riding

October 2005

Monday 10 — Wicked
Thanksgiving Day CAN

Tuesday 11

Wednesday 12
Horse of the Year Show begins

Thursday 13

Friday 14

Saturday 15

Sunday 16 — Rent
Horse of the Year Show ends

- Check water troughs for leaves
- Clip if necessary

October 2005

Monday 17 Nc Pd

Tuesday 18

Wednesday 19

Thursday 20

Friday 21

Saturday 22 Planted 40 conifers along back and side. (£40 owed to J from B)

Sunday 23 Rent Paid

- Beware of grazing conditions that are likely to induce laminitis (p.25)
- Increase feed and give hay (p.34)

October 2005

Monday 24 — ~~Nc Pd~~ Nc Pd

Tuesday 25

Wednesday 26

Thursday 27

Friday 28

Saturday 29 — Changed to Winter Side -

Sunday 30 — Rub Raid

British Summer Time ends

- Administer wormer, particularly for tapeworm (p.13)

MONTH
Weather very mild   Ave Daily temp 15
                     Ave Night temp 10

November

In the outward appearance, riding should present itself as an art. Horse and rider in all movements should give the impression of two living creatures merged into one.

Alois Podhajsky *The Complete Training of Horse and Rider*

October/ November 2005

Monday 31 — Hallowe'en
Nc Pd
Rent Paid up to.

Tuesday 1
£130 monthly rent
£100 L chg + £30 pst
(months money)
+ carrots x 2 Pd
£40 owed to K for Jakes rug. Pd

Wednesday 2

Thursday 3

Friday 4

Saturday 5 — Equine Event

Sunday 6 — Equine Event
Rnt Pd

● Keep a check for mud fever (p.29), rainscald (p.30), thrush (p.24)

November 2005

Monday 7 Nc Pd

Tuesday 8

Wednesday 9 FARRIER

Thursday 10

Friday 11

Saturday 12

1st cold weather. night. (°3)

Sunday 13 Remembrance Sunday

Pushed over to ½ side winter.

- Look out for frozen water troughs

November 2005

Monday 14 Nc Pd.

Tuesday 15

Wednesday 16

Thursday 17

Friday 18

Saturday 19

Sunday 20 Rwt Pd

- Laminitis can still occur in suspectible horses (p.25)

November 2005

Monday 21 Nc Pd

Tuesday 22

Wednesday 23

Thursday 24   Thanksgiving Day USA

Friday 25

Saturday 26

Sunday 27   Rut Pd

● Administer wormer, particularly for bots (or December) (p.13)

November/December 2005

Monday 28 — Nc Pd

Tuesday 29

Wednesday 30 — Rent Pd up to.

Thursday 1 — NEW CONTRACT £32 per week new rent   LPd   KPd
£138.66 per month chq(L)

Friday 2 — £138.66 Pd   £38.66 Pd to L from pot.

Saturday 3

Sunday 4 — Rent Pd

- Monitor your horse's weight (p.34), increasing hay and feed if necessary
- On freezing mornings give extra hay to grass-kept horses

November weather mixed

December

Horses, it always seems
To me, are half a dream, even when
You have them under your hand...

Christopher Fry *Venus Observed*

December 2005

Monday 5   Nc Pd

Tuesday 6

Wednesday 7

Thursday 8

Friday 9

Saturday 10

Sunday 11   Rut Pd

- Keep a check for mud fever (p.29), rainscald (p.30), thrush (p.24)
- Look out for frozen water troughs

December 2005

Monday 12 Nc Pd

Tuesday 13

Wednesday 14

Thursday 15 Olympia begins

Friday 16

Saturday 17

Sunday 18 Rub Pd

● Watch out for rug rubs, adjusting fit if necessary

December 2005

Monday 19 — Nc Pd — Olympia ends

Tuesday 20

Wednesday 21 Fainer.

Thursday 22

Friday 23

Saturday 24

Sunday 25 Rnt Paid — Christmas Day

- Administer wormer, particularly for bots (p.13)

December/January 2005/6

Monday 26 — Boxing Day
Nc Pd.

Tuesday 27 — Bank Holiday UK

Wednesday 28
50 Bales hay from Derek. @ £2.40p
£120 (Kairina pd)

Thursday 29

Friday 30

Saturday 31 — New Year's Eve
Rent Pd up to

Sunday 1 — New Year's Day
£138.66 31/1/06
Rent Pd 31/1/06

K = Pd pd. (hay) transfer
L. Wormed

- Monitor your horse's weight (p.34), increasing hay and feed if necessary

Dec weather very cold - not much rain.
Lost approx 15 bales of hay from June deli[very]

January 2006

Rnt Pd

Monday 2 — 1

Tuesday 3

Wednesday 4

Thursday 5

Friday 6

Saturday 7

Sunday 8

- On freezing mornings give extra hay to grass-kept horses

FARRIER 8th FEB 06. (WED)

Useful Addresses

Equine associations, shows and fairs UK

British Dressage, National Agricultural Centre, Stoneleigh Park, Warwickshire CV8 2RJ. Tel. 024 76698830; Fax. 024 76690390. www.britishdressage.co.uk

British Eventing, National Agricultural Centre, Stoneleigh Park, Warwickshire CV8 2LR. Tel. 024 7669 8856; Fax. 024 7669 7235. www.britisheventing.co.uk

British Equestrian Trade Association, East Wing, Stockeld Park, Wetherby, West Yorkshire LS22 4AW. www.beta-uk.org

British Horse Society, Stoneleigh Deer Park, Kenilworth, Warwickshire CV8 2XZ. Tel. 08701 202 244; Fax. 01926 707 800. www.bhs.org.uk
The BHS is the largest equine charity in Britain. It is dedicated to improving the welfare of horses and ponies through education and can supply information on a wide range of equestrian subjects.

British Show Jumping Association, National Agricultural Centre, Stoneleigh Park, Warwickshire CV8 2LR. Tel. 024 7669 8800; Fax. 024 7669 6685. www.bsja.co.uk

Contour Exhibitions and Events Limited, Suite 7, Swallow Court, Devonshire Gate, Tiverton, Devon EX16 7EJ. Tel. 01884 841644/841925; Fax. 01884 841647. www.contour.net
Details of the four equine fairs held in Britain each year: South West, North of England, Scottish, Midlands.

Veteran Horse Society, Hendre Fawr Farm, St Dogmaels, Cardigan, SA43 3LZ. Tel. 01239 881300; Fax. 01239 881310. www.veteran-horse-society.co.uk

Equine businesses and general websites

www.adas.co.uk Head office ADAS Wolverhampton HQ, Woodthorne, Wergs Road, Wolverhampton WV6 8TQ. Consultancies and research centres throughout England and Wales. Tel. 0845 766 0085. The ADAS (Agricultural Development Advisory Service) can help with soil and feed analysis and other equine management issues.

www.horseandhound.co.uk Details of all sorts of horsey events, etc.

www.horseit.com Useful website with plenty of information on horse care and links to other horsey sites.

www.horsetrace.com Horsetrace Ltd, Armyn Cross, Minety, Wiltshire SN16 9RJ. Tel. 0845 644 2000. This organization offers ways for you to find information about your horse and helps to trace stolen horses.

Equine associations, shows and fairs US

Kentucky Horse Park, 4089 Iron Works Parkway, Lexington, Kentucky KY 40511. Tel. 859 233 4303 (TDD), 800 678 8813 (toll free); Fax. 859 254 0253. www.imh.org/khp The horse park is a working horse farm and museum dedicated to the relationship between man and the horse. The website has links to a vast number of equestrian organizations, clubs, magazines, etc.

National Future Farmers of America (FFA) Center, PO Box 68960, 6060 FFA Drive, Indianapolis IN 46268-0960. Tel. 317 802 6060; Fax. 317 802 6061. www.ffa.org. The FFA has details of the Horse Proficiency Program and other information.

The American Horse Council, 1616 H Street NW, 7th Floor, Washington DC 20006. Tel. 202 296 4031; Fax. 202 296 1970. www.horsecouncil.org/ahc.html The American Horse Council represents all aspects of the US equine industry and can sell you a Horse Industry Directory, which lists breed and performance associations.

United States Equestrian Team, Pottersville Road, PO Box 355, Gladstone, New Jersey NJ 07934. Tel. 908 234 1251; Fax. 908 234 9417. www.uset.com A non-profit-making organization providing training, equipment and finance to skilled equestrians to enable them to enter major international competitions.

United States Pony Clubs, Inc, 4041 Iron Works Parkway, Lexington, Kentucky KY 40511-8462. Tel. 859 254 7669; Fax. 859 233 4652. www.ponyclub.org

4-H, National 4-H Headquarters, 1400 Independence Avenue SW, Washington DC 20250-2225 www.national4-hheadquarters.gov

Equine health

Equilibrium Products Ltd, Unit 7 Upper Wingbury Farm, Leighton Road, Wingrave, Buckinghamshire HP22 4LW. Tel. 01296 682681; Fax. 01296 680345. www.equilibriumproducts.com
Manufacturers of muzzle nets for headshakers.

Equine Grass Sickness Fund, Moredun Foundation, Pentlands Science Park, Penicuik, Midlothian EH26 0PZ. Tel. 0131 445 6257; Fax. 0131 445 6235. www.grasssickness.org.uk
Research into grass sickness and information and support for owners of horses that contract the disease.

Horses & Courses Ltd, Crawley Grange, North Crawley, Buckinghamshire MK16 9HL. Tel. 01727 751133; Fax. 08707 065295. www.horsesandcourses.co.uk
Correspondence college offering short courses in horse-related subjects.

Palm's Rest,
Arlington Close, Undy, Monmouthshire NP26 3EF.
Tel. 0871 717 9808; Fax. 0871 717 9809.
www.equinefarewells.com
A service offering equine funerals.

The Laminitis Trust
Helpline Tel. 0905 105 105 1 (calls cost £1 per minute).
www.laminitis.org Information about laminitis prevention, treatment, drug trials and much more.

www.liv.ac.uk/sarcoids A website devoted to providing information on sarcoids and their treatment. Linked to the Division of Equine Studies, University of Liverpool.

Equine charities UK

Ada Cole Rescue Stables, Broadlands, Broadley Common, Near Nazeing, Waltham Abbey, Essex EN9 2DH. Tel. 01992 892133; Fax. 01992 893841.
www.adacole.co.uk

Blue Cross Head Office, Shilton Road, Burford, Oxfordshire OX18 4PF. Tel. 01993 825500; Fax. 01993 823083. www.bluecross.org.uk

Brooke Hospital for Animals, Broadmead House, 21 Panton Street, London SW1Y 4DR. Tel. 020 7930 0210; Fax. 020 7930 2386. www.brookehospital.com

Heavy Horse Rest & Rescue, Plas y Gwynt, Llanfaethlu, Isle of Anglesey LL65 4PA. Tel. 01407 730757. www.heavyhorserestandrescue.com

Home of Rest for Horses, Westcroft Stables, Speen Farm, Slad Lane, Princes Risborough, Buckinghamshire HP27 0PP. Tel.01494 488 464; Fax. 01494 488 767. www.homeofrestforhorses.co.uk

Horses and Ponies Protection Association, The Stables, Burnley Wharf, Manchester Road, Burnley, Lancashire BB11 1JZ. Tel. 01282 455992; Fax. 01282 451992. www.happa.org.uk

International League for the Protection of Horses, Anne Colvin House, Snetterton, Norfolk NR16 2LR. Tel. 0870 870 1927; Fax. 0870 904 1927. www.ilph.org Cruelty Hotline: Tel. 0870 871 1927.

Redwings Horse Sanctuary, Hapton, Norwich NR15 1SP. Tel. 01508 481000; Fax. 0870 458 1947. Welfare Hotline: Tel. 01508 481008. www.redwings.co.uk

The Donkey Sanctuary, Slade House Farm, Salcombe Regis, Sidmouth, Devon EX10 0NU.

Book clubs

The Equestrian Society
Brunel House, Newton Abbot, Devon, TQ12 1BR
Call: 0870 4422123
Fax: 0870 2255025

Equestrian's Edge
6650 East 60th Street
PO Box 6325
Indianapolis, IN 46206
www.equestriansedge.com

Equine charities US

American Horse Defense Fund,
11206 Valley View Drive, Kensington MD 20895.
Tel. 1 866 983 3456 (toll free). www.ahdf.org

California Equine Retirement Foundation,
34033 Kooden Road, Winchester, California CA 92596.
Tel. 909 926 4190; Fax. 909 926 4181.
www.cerfhorses.org

Equine Rescue League Inc.,
PO Box 4366, Leesburg, Virginia VA 20177.
Tel. 703 771 1240. www.equinerescueleague.org

Hooved Animal Humane Society,
PO Box 400, 10804 McConnell Road, Woodstock, Illinois IL 60098. Tel. 815 337 5563; Fax. 815 337 5569.
www.hahs.org

Horse Rescue and Relief Retirement Fund Inc.,
1768 Newt Green Road, Cumming, Georgia GA 30040.
Tel. 770 886 5419. www.savethehorses.org

Thoroughbred Retirement Foundation,
450 Shrewsbury Plaza, Shrewsbury, New Jersey NJ 07702-4332. www.trfinc.org

Riding charities UK

Fortune Centre of Riding Therapy,
Avon Tyrell, Bransgore, Christchurch, Dorset BH23 8EE.
Tel. 01425 673297; Fax. 01425 674320.
www.fortunecentre.org An organization using horses and riding to help young people with behavioural problems.

Mark Davies Injured Riders Fund,
38 Regent on the River, William Morris Way, London SW6 2UT. Tel./Fax. 0207 736 1738. www.mdirf.co.uk

Riding For the Disabled Association,
Lavinia Norfolk House, Avenue R, Stoneleigh Park, Warwickshire CV8 2LY. Tel. 024 7669 6510;
Fax. 024 7669 6532.
www.riding-for-disabled.org.uk

Riding charities US

www.equisearch.com As well as general horsey information, this site provides information on a number of organizations offering therapeutic riding for disabled riders or those requiring special facilities.

Equine associations AUS and NZ

The Australian Pony Club Council Inc.,
National Secretariat: PO Box 206
TWEED HEADS 2485
www.ponyclub-australia.org

Australian Veterinary Association,
PO Box 371, Artarmon, NSW 1570
www.ava.com.au

New Zealand Veterinary Association,
PO Box 11-212, Manners Street, Wellington
www.vets.org.nz